Go Home and Do the Washing!

Three Centuries of Pioneering Bristol Women

Go Home and Do the Washing!

Three Centuries of Pioneering Bristol Women

Lorna Brierley and Helen Reid

L.B. to my Grand daughter
Sarah.

"The prevailing manners of an age depend more than we are aware, or are willing to allow, on the conduct of the women; this is one of the principle hinges on which the the great machine of human society turns."

(*Hannah More, 1777*)

Acknowledgements

Of the many who have helped us with the research into this book,
we are especially grateful to the following:

Bristol University Library
John Casson
Beryl Corner
Mary Dixon
Maggie Lane
Owen Reid
Ruth Trapnell

Cover photographs from left to right:

**Elizabeth Casson, Annie Kenny, Clara Butt,
Hannah More, Marian Pease, Susanna Winkworth**

Printed in the UK by Cromwell Press, Trowbridge, Wilts

Cover Design: Juliet Clarke and Sally Mundy
Book Design: Sally Mundy

Contents

Introduction

Women have always contributed substantially to the economic, social and cultural life of Bristol, particularly in the field of the arts, education, medicine and philanthropy, but the history books leave them out, apart from dutiful references to Hannah More and Mary Carpenter.

A trawl through the late 18th century street directories reveals a startling number of businesses run by women, who plied most unexpected trades. In *Sketchley's Directory* of 1775, for example, 250 of the (paid for) entries are for women. In *Matthews Directory* 1793-4, 274 women are listed as working in the city. Women were pursuing over 90 different trades.

The frontispiece of Matthew's 1793-4 Street Directory

The majority were working in areas where you would expect to find women: they were landladies of inns and taverns, they ran shops, or kept lodging houses, combining as always, business and family obligations. A significant number worked in fashion, as dressmakers or milliners, and in teaching, or running private 'academies'.

The next biggest category is retailing, and in the late 18th century, women ran grocery shops, bakeries and confectionery shops and even china and tea warehouses - often the two were combined.

But here the surprises start, for the 1775 list includes two women poulterers, eight butchers, two fishmongers, a corn factor and a cheese-monger, five corn chandlers and six upholsterers. Even more startling were the woman midwife and an apothecary (in an age when men only were allowed to practice), a plumber, an organ builder, a wine-maker, a tobacconist, two soap-makers, a cork cutter, two gardeners, a watch-maker, a smith, two tinplate workers, a basket maker and a brushmaker, a printer (Sarah Farley who took over her late husband's newspaper, the Journal), a stationer, a limeburner, a rope maker, a sexton, three brokers, a bookseller, a wine merchant and a hallier (carter).

Plainly some of these businesses were run by widows of the original trader, and the women employed men to do the work - but nevertheless there seemed to be no gender barrier to running a traditionally male business. Women were thought fit to belong to the commercial classes, and worked without hindrance from city by-laws, or restrictions by the Merchant Venturers, trade organisations or guilds. There seemed to be no social stigma either, or these women would not have paid to be listed in the commercial directories.

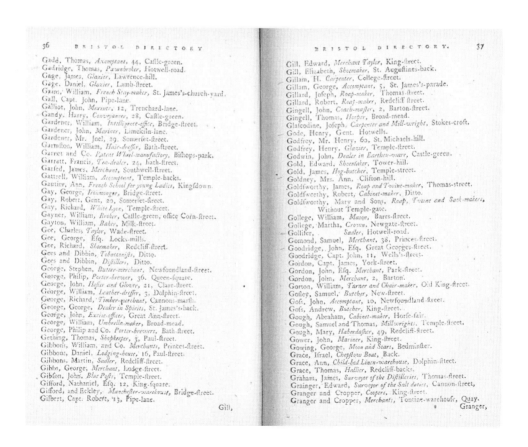

A page from the 1793 directory listing women's occupations.

Almost 20 years later, the *Matthews Directory* of 1793-4 shows the same widespread of occupations for women. Again, the public houses, lodgings and retail trade account for the majority of women listed, but here too are surprises: four were cabinet makers, one ran a tripehouse, there were two house painters, a tyler and plasterer, a landscaper, a seedshop keeper, two brightsmiths, two tobacco pipe manufacturers, a ship's chandler, two stay (sail) makers, a wharfinger (dock worker), two saddlers, a currier, a wine worker, a timber dealer, three ironmongers, two keepers of circulating libraries, a wheelwright, a farrier, a pump and blockmaker. It is a list that the Equal Opportunities Commission would be proud of today, and it does not even include the many influential women involved in the philanthropic and charitable work for which the city had always been famous, or in the educational and spiritual work of the non-conformist religious movement that dominated Bristol life.

Clearly up to Regency times, Bristol women made a significant contribution to the economic health of the city, but analysis of the street directories 50 years on show strikingly that the enterprising merchant class of women had virtually disappeared, at a time when the population of the city had practically doubled.

The 1853 *Matthews Directory* shows that the working class women were still working as landladies and lodging house keepers, and in the retail and clothing trades, and many more, unlisted, were by then working in the factories created by the Industrial Revolution, at Wills tobacco factory, or for Fry's. They were making pins, weaving cotton or making shoes. Another army of working class women was by then employed as servants for the newly rich middle class.

But the choice of work had shrunk; by 1854 there are only 40 trades listed for women, and most of these are the traditional feminine ones: women were working as milliners, haberdashers, mantua makers, (dressmakers) and hairdressers.

The reason is easy to find; Bristol's merchant class had become gentrified. The merchants had become upwardly mobile, they had bought grand houses in Clifton and, later, villas in Redland, and their wives and daughters had to be educated to become ladies and to marry into the class above. Work for them was out of the question, and running a business became a male domain. The only possible occupation for less wealthy genteel women were in teaching, the arts and philanthropy; any connection with trade was frowned on.

The 1853 directory shows the extent to which jobs had been allotted genders. There are no women at all listed as working in the professions; they were no longer running artisan businesses, there were fewer women butchers, bakers, more men were now landlords of taverns and public houses, and women had become employees, not entrepreneurs.

So the commercial list for 1853 shows few surprises; there is a woman dealer in baby linen, a bookseller, one or two butchers and bakers, a dyer, and a fruiterer; the one entirely female occupation listed is a laundress. Real men did not wash and iron in 1854! There were a handful of women brokers, meaning that they sold second-hand clothes or furniture, three pawnbrokers, and a number of lacemakers. Otherwise the largest category of women's work is that of teaching: non-scientific subjects such as music, drawing and French and so on, and that of keeping a school.

Yet historians of the Women's movement always cite Bristol as a strong-hold of feminism in the 19th century, and with good reason. The city acted as a nursery for several important women's movements that improved women's education, opened up careers in the professions, in civic representation, and eventually led to the vote. Bristol women first launched a number of national campaigns: Quakers started a Clifton Ladies Anti-Slavery Society in 1840, several Bristol women signed the first-ever women's suffrage petition in 1866, and the Bristol suffrage society was only the fifth to be formed in the country. They were also vigorously active in setting up local strike support committees in the 1880s, which lead to the Association for the Promotion of Trades Unions among Women in 1889.

Since they could not participate in the public life of the city or in local government, or join any of the men-only business, political or cultural institutions that ran the city, radical women of the middle class - often supported by private means - worked behind the scenes through various charitable societies: alleviating poverty, improving health and literacy, running missions and schools, setting up working girls clubs for health and education. For their own daughters there was the Association for the Promotion of Higher Education of Women, founded in 1869.

Other quieter ways in which women gained influence were by serving on school boards, or as guardians administering the Poor Law. They were great founders and joiners of Associations for women.

It was thanks to Mary Clifford, who in 1882 was one of the first four women Poor Law Guardians to be elected in Bristol, that the National Council of Women was formed. She was its first president. Reformer Mary Carpenter played a large role in the setting up of the National Association for the Promotion of Social Science, and Anna Maria Priestman established the Bristol Association of Working Women.

The link between feminism and politics was made in 1881 when Emily Sturge founded the first women-only political organisation in the country, the Bristol Women's Liberal Association. It aimed "to diffuse knowledge on political questions of general and local interest", and hoped to interest working women in politics. It also refused to support political candidates who did not take a firm line on women's suffrage.

The same names crop up again and again in different contexts: the Priestman sisters, Mary Estlin, the Sturges, the Winkworths, Florence Hill, Dr. Eliza Dunbar. It is clear that they were all networkers long before the word was invented, supporting each other's causes and gathering male supporters who could give their campaigns a higher profile.

The Contagious Diseases Act

It says a lot for the courage of these middle-class Victorian Bristol women that they also supported Josephine Butler and her long fight against the unfair Contagious Diseases Act. It had been introduced in the 1860s to try to control the spread of venereal disease among soldiers and sailors, and gave police wide-ranging powers to lock up any woman suspected of being a prostitute for up to three months and be subjected to internal examinations against her will. The national fight against the act began in Bristol, when three non-conformist women invited Josephine Butler to speak at a debate at the Social Science annual Congress in 1869. They became leaders of a national campaign to repeal an Act which women of their class were not even supposed to know about, let alone discuss.

Ironically, because of the delicacy of the subject, women were barred from the subsequent Bristol debate on the Contagious Diseases Act on the grounds that only medical professionals could take part. It was a triumph for women and for Bristol in particular that the Bristol-born Elizabeth Blackwell, the first British woman to qualify as a doctor (albeit via an American qualification) was the only woman allowed to attend. The Act was finally suspended in 1882. Women had to wait until the 20th Century for the major reforms that changed their lives radically - the vote, entry to universities, equal pay.

Bristol women have come a long way since the days of their struggling 18th and 19th century sisters. Most of the women celebrated in this book were pioneers in their fields who had to work against the social grain of the times in order to succeed. They were the social workers, reformers and educators who helped shape the identity of the great city of Bristol, and in this book we acknowledge them at last.

An early photograph of 1862 showing vagrant street children

1 The Reformers and their Religious Background

An apparently peaceful sewing class for the girls of the Red Lodge, Park Row, Bristol.

Before the welfare state existed, charity, the Poor Law Guardians and an army of worthy women took its place, and wealthy Bristol was always famous for its many ancient endowed and municipal charities.

The earliest charitable foundations had involved women: often the wife of the Mayor was designated to oversee the day to day running of a charitable institution, especially if it was a school or an almshouse for females.

The other great motivator was religion; the strong non-conformist tradition in Bristol produced generations of women whose faith dictated that they go out and do something practical for the less fortunate.

In the 19th century the Anglican church too encouraged legions of middle-class women to do something positive to alleviate poverty, drunkenness and ignorance. If the tone was sometimes patronising, the intention was good, and hundreds of charitable societies were set up to encourage temperance and church-going, and to provide clothing, food, blankets or firewood to the thousands of families who lived in abject poverty in Bristol's dockside slums.

The result was a kind of ad hoc social work, with the well-off middle-class women going into lowly homes to teach domestic economy, cooking and cleaning - a little rich from women who employed servants. But it was donations from women such as these that sustained institutions like the Clifton Dispensary, which gave free medical help to those presenting a chit.

The fact that the poor had to ask for charity, and be grateful, often soured the social transaction and the great weakness was of course the Victorian attitude that only the deserving should be helped. It was the undeserving that needed it most, as the Quakers realised.

It was the same charitable and enlightened women who strove to improve education for girls and further education for women, with lecture courses, evening classes for factory and shop girls, and basic education for young children, at Sunday schools.
The social awareness that came from carrying out charity work had the effect of raising their consciousness, and it is no coincidence that Bristol the charitable city was also the home of some of the earliest women's movements. These same charitable ladies became the champions of women's emancipation, as we shall see.

Mary Carpenter (1807 - 1877)

Mary Carpenter is known not only in Bristol but also internationally for her work among the deprived and delinquent children of the streets. In the teeth of official obstruction and public horror at her non-sectarian views on the education of children, Mary Carpenter held doggedly to her conviction that there was no such thing as a child that could not be reclaimed from a criminal destiny if given food, an education leading also to a trade, and shown sufficient love. She also felt that the child's family was almost always a better environment for the growing child than an institution, and that whatever crimes the child may have committed, its debt to society was far outweighed by the debt society owed the child. These views were the guiding principles of a lifetime of extraordinary achievement and devotion to children. These were extraordinarily radical views for her day. A century and a half later such views can still be denounced as dangerously 'soft on crime' by leader writers whipping up public indignation in the popular press.

The first ten years of Mary's life were, by all accounts, extremely happy. Her parents, Dr Lant Carpenter and Anna Penn, married on Christmas Day in 1805, following Lant's appointment as Unitarian Minister at St George's Meeting, Exeter. Mary was born in 1807, the first of six children, three girls and three boys. The home was simple, scrupulously neat and clean, and a model of such mutual self-service and kindness between the family members, that they held to each other in great devotion to the end of their days. Mary, especially, adored her preacher father, and wanted all her life to be true to his inspiration.

Both Lant and Anna had experience in teaching: he had tutored in a wide range of subjects since his graduation in theology at Glasgow University, and on marriage they admitted seven boys as pupils into their home. He seemed to have been an affectionate, gentle and inspiring teacher, his wife a woman of tremendous energy and organising capabilities. Thus was a pattern established which was to last until Mary was forty, sowing the seeds for her own career as educationalist and reformer.

In 1817 Lant Carpenter was invited to become Minister at Lewin's Mead Meeting in Bristol. The family moved to a new home in 2 Great George Street, a house large enough to accommodate a boarding school for boys. Here Philip, the last child in the family, was born in 1819, evoking tender affection and care from Mary, an affection that later she would show to all deprived and neglected children. Mary and her sister Anna became pupils in their father's school, thus receiving an excellent education in subjects which were unusual fare for girls in their day, and are now incorporated in the National Curriculum: science, including the new discipline of geology with its exciting - yet religiously disturbing - revision of the age of the world, mathematics, English literature, history, geography and modern languages. Mary also loved the beauty of painting and poetry although she rarely allowed herself to indulge in either. Intelligent girls born later in the century, such as the Sturge sisters, would have envied this intellectual feast.

A fellow-pupil was James Martineau who became Mary's life-long friend. Although two years older than Mary they shared lessons, and while still in their teens successfully took over the class when Lant became incapacitated by 'exhaustion'; one of several episodes of a depressive illness, perhaps contributed to by an excessive work-load. The workload of helping to run the school must in turn have been excessive for the sixteen year old girl and in 1821 Mary fell ill with acute rheumatism and agonising iritis, threatening her with blindness. As she slowly recovered she yearned to be of even more use to her father, whose health was deteriorating.

James Martineau had left the school at this time and the burden on Lant was great. Three years after her illness Mary became an assistant to her father and developed her considerable ability as a teacher. Nevertheless nearly three years later Lant suffered a complete breakdown and, with a friend, set off on a sea-voyage to Hyères in the South of France where he was to spend the winter. Anna Carpenter invited James Martineau to return to run the school and to become Minister until Lant's recovery. For a while the two young people worked together and at their own studies. In spite of anxiety about her adored father this must have been a period of great satisfaction to Mary. But it was not to last. Mary was sent by her mother to be a governess to girls in the Isle of Wight, and spent a miserable year there until Lant Carpenter, improved in health, returned in 1828 and brought her home.

It may be assumed that this period of exile was the family's way of separating Mary from James: in her later writings she indicated an unrequited affection. For a short while she was at home with her father and with James before being dispatched to a further and happier post as governess.

The Carpenters had hoped that James would take over the school from Lant. It was when he refused that they first learnt of his engagement to the daughter of a Unitarian Minister in Derby. In the event the Carpenters' school for boys was closed to be replaced in 1829 by a girls' boarding school run by Mrs Carpenter, Mary and her sister Anna. Mary did not enjoy teaching the Y.Ls as she privately called the young ladies: "I long to leave behind me something which men would not willingly let die, something which would enable my thoughts to mingle with my fellow beings when I am lying in death. But this is a hope little suited to my powers."

In 1839 Lant had a further and more serious breakdown. His son, Russell, recently graduated in theology, returned to take over Lewin's Mead Meeting. Lant's depression, with marked thoughts of guilt and unworthiness, was so severe that the services of Dr John Freeman were obtained and the two men set off for Europe. Reports were received of gradual mental improvement: eight month's later on a voyage from Naples to Rome Lant was reported missing on a stormy night, during which poor Dr Freeman had been incapacitated by sea-sickness. The body was recovered three months later. It was never clear what had happened to Lant that night.

Mary now in her early thirties, devastated by this appalling loss, was seriously depressed for the next two years. With great courage she continued to carry out her duties in the school with the help of her sister Anna. Eventually her mother, fearing for her state of mind, sent her for a period of travel in Europe with two companions with resulting improvement in mental health. However in 1844 she had a further attack of acute rheumatism forcing her to give up teaching. During this time she compiled a book of 'Morning and Evening Meditations' which sold well in America and Britain. This led to her first meeting and ultimate friendship with Lady Byron, who had become an eccentric philanthropist living with utmost frugality in order to be able to devote revenues from her scandalous late husband's estate to good causes. She was to support Mary's projects as long as she lived, and was the benefactress of the Red Lodge.

In 1848, that year of revolutions in Europe, there came a fundamental change in Mary's life. She was now aged forty. Her sister Anna, two years younger, got married and the couple took over the main house in Great George Street, with Mary and her mother inhabiting the annexe. This finally brought about the closure of the boarding-school and Mary, who encouraged by her father had long espoused the anti-slavery cause, wrote that she was at last "free of the shackles" imposed on her since girlhood.

Two years previously she had opened a 'ragged school' in a room in a tenement house in Lewin's Mead where she gave what little time she had to help the hard-pressed, untrained and barely paid teacher. The boys and girls who attended at will were ragged, filthy and completely wild. Mary was convinced that if they only had a warm place to stay during the day, where they could be fed and taught the basics of reading and writing, and thereby shown an alternative life to their experience on the streets, they could be saved from prison. This was then the inevitable fate of such street children, a fate from which they generally emerged, not reformed, but criminalised. She felt a great desire " To make them feel they are not forgotten, nor beasts; that they too will be men." Unlike Hannah More she had no intention of limiting their education to their 'station' and felt that their education should be the best possible: "It is a mistake to imagine that because the children are ragged, the education need be ragged also." She also tried - in vain - to do away with the pejorative title 'ragged school'.

Such a tremendous task had little popular support, especially from the city authorities. But the Unitarian congregation in Bristol, although only 700 strong, were generous. Trained teachers were essential and a Mr Andrews and his sister were appointed, both experienced in teaching deprived children, appreciating that each one was an individual worthy of respect. By the time Mary was free to teach in the school full-time it had moved to a disused mission chapel in the slums of St James' Back - a dangerous area in which to work. The police, initially hostile, became supportive, so much so that one of them was reported for neglect of duty, having been two hours in the ragged school setting copies for the boys.

The school became one for all ages: infants and juniors in the mornings, boys and girls for shoemaking and sewing in the afternoons and the long-standing evening classes for young people. Here Mary established the principles of education which she continued to put into practice in later years and about which she wrote in endless pamphlets and books. She was totally opposed to corporal punishment, neither this nor "shame or ridicule should be made use of; discipline must be maintained by firmness, order and kindness."

What was even more shocking for the city authorities, and ensured that Mary struggled for financial support for her schools almost to the end of her life, was that non-sectarian religion was taught, the children's interest captured by simple Bible stories. Perhaps the essence of Mary's teaching was that she started from the point at which she could stir imagination and interest - "from the known towards the unknown".

Teaching methods which are commonplace in the infant school of today were developed at a time when teaching consisted of rote learning, with discipline maintained by the cane. Geology, science, stories, drama, play and singing were all grist to her mill, and a great emphasis was also laid on the pleasure of beauty, wherever it could be found. Soap and towels were provided by Mrs Carpenter and gradually the untamed children became sufficiently clean and orderly to be taken to the Zoo or to the Museum.

During this time Mary studied the problem of juvenile delinquency; reading and visiting penal institutions where children as young as seven were confined. She gave evidence to a Select Committee of the House of Commons appointed to inquire into the question of Criminal and Destitute children. Mary came up against the 'hard-liners' of the day who believed in solitary confinement as a first step, with flogging and, until 1852, transportation for repeated offences.

While the debate continued, Mary was anxious to do more for these children. John Wesley's old school in Kingswood became vacant. The house was provided by Russell Scott of Bath and furnished with the assistance of Lady Byron and other subscribers so that Mary could try her experiment of a reformatory school. In September 1852 the school was opened to accept ten boys and five girls aged 8 to 14: some were delinquent, others seriously disturbed. Mary was not altogether happy with the master and matron and, in order to oversee the well-being of the children she would walk the four miles to Kingswood each afternoon whatever the weather, and later walk back to the night school at St James' Back.

Mary's personal finances were fairly meagre: when Lant Carpenter died his estate was left to his wife. Thus, unlike Hannah More with an annuity to give her independence, Mary remained totally dependent on her mother, who despite her anxiety and puzzlement that her daughter should work in such dangerous surroundings, nevertheless supported her with great affection to the end of her life. There is, however, nothing to suggest that Mary had a generous allowance, although it is certain that she spent the minimum on herself in order to provide more for her needy children and their families.

It soon became evident that Mary's dream of reformation in a family-type home at Kingswood was unrealistic. Many children did well but others, especially the older girls already accustomed to the physical and sexual freedom of the streets, were uncontrollable. The school was reorganised as a reformatory for boys, and this only emphasised the need for provision for girls. Once more Lady Byron came to the rescue by purchasing the Red Lodge in Park Row in Bristol. Mary installed herself as Superintendent, with a resident matron.

Even those experienced in dealing with delinquent and disturbed girls in the 20th century would have quailed from the task undertaken by Mary. The girls were from deprived and criminal backgrounds who had known no discipline or only that of fear and brutality; often hungry, dirty, usually diseased, often with impetigo, and, more seriously, tuberculosis. Many had had several prison sentences. Mary reached for what was lovable in all children and many of these pathetic creatures responded to her care. Others, especially the older girls, continued to steal, to abscond and behave in ways that taxed the staff to the utmost. Mary, driven by an inner need to work unceasingly, showed infinite patience towards the children but expected the impossible of the Matron and teachers, driving them as pitilessly as she drove herself.

Mary prepared for the first Christmas at Red Lodge as well as at Kingswood. Each establishment was to have a Christmas tree with a present from Mary for each child. At St James' Back a dinner was planned for two hundred children. Daily, Mary walked between the three schools, and this after working and writing at home from an early hour in the morning. Not surprisingly before Christmas she collapsed with a further attack of rheumatic fever and lay dangerously ill for three months, to be nursed devotedly by her mother.

In spite of her heart being affected, Mary struggled to get back to work and by May was once more able to go out of doors. Mary's statement in the introduction to her book on Reformatory Schools (1851) can stand to-day:

It is not needed, at the present day, to demonstrate the immense impor-tance of the juvenile portion of the community to the future, and even to the present welfare of the state, or to show the need of education to prepare the young to be good citizens and useful members of society.

To this end the curriculum for the girls comprised reading, writing and simple arithmetic as well as regular non-sectarian religious instruction. In addition there was tuition in geography, a knowledge of general affairs and singing. Industrial training included knitting, needlework and several hours daily in household work. Laundering and cooking were taught so that older girls would be enabled to enter domestic service. A number did well and householders would have been fortunate to receive such well-trained servants. However the Reports available show that there were many problems with unruly girls and untrained, badly paid staff. Mary criticised staff for lack of control and harshness but sympathy is due to them in what was often an impossible task.

A Miss Bathurst was appointed as Mary's assistant and she proved competent but eventually her health broke down. Difficulties continued, only balanced by success with younger children who responded to Mary's affection. Finally after five turbulent years a Mrs Johnson was appointed in 1859, a remarkably capable woman who ignored Mary's instructions when necessary. A trial of strength took place only solved by the intervention of Mr Turner, the Inspector, who must have shown great skill in reconciling two very determined women. Mary was able to accept the situation when she saw it was for the benefit of the children but gradually withdrew from the management of Red Lodge and prof-itably used the time to work for penal reform.

In 1856 Mrs Carpenter died and for a while Mary was given a home by her sister Anna and her husband. But her dream and prayers for a home of her own was made possible once again by the generosity of Lady Bryon. Two houses were bought in Park Row: one, the Cottage, now demolished, was adjacent to Red Lodge, providing a stepping-stone for girls as they prepared to leave the school for home or work in Bristol. The second house, for Mary, still stands on the corner of Park Row and Lodge Street. Here she set up home and within two years a second dream came true: she adopted Roseanna, aged 5, thought to be an orphan and found in failing health in a workhouse. The difference between Mary's practical philanthropy and that of the famous Pastor Muller was shown by the fact that the child was refused admittance to the Muller Orphanages as she "could not produce evidence that she had been born in wedlock." She was the joy of Mary's life and remained with Mary for a number of years until completing her education in a boarding-school, after which she returned to keep house for Mary.

Once Mary was installed in Red Lodge House with little Roseanna she felt the need for a further assistant, and Lady Byron provided one. Then followed a period of tragi-comedy with the advent of Frances Power Cobbe in 1858, the daughter of an Anglo-Irish landowner. Frances Cobbe was eccentric, stout, hospitable and well-travelled, and now at the age of 36 she sought a woman's companionship and love. We cannot imagine what picture Lady Byron had given of Mary, but the two women could hardly have been more dissimilar. Frances was soon full of admiration for Mary's achievements and did all she could to share the uncongenial work. However she had envisaged a woman with whom she could exchange confidences, discuss religion, literature and, indeed, anything other than Mary's constant preoccupations with the Red Lodge School or St James' Back. There is an account of Mary allowing friends to talk while she struggled, breathless, up Christmas Steps. Once at the top she resumed her monologue about the children.

Frances made emotional demands on Mary which were regularly rebuffed. Frances must have endured much: she had put up with hardships while travelling alone in the near East on a mule and camping in the desert, but she was a bon viveur, used to space and lively company, not to living in a street and subsisting on Mary's diet of cold salt beef. (The diet for the growing girls was equally spartan and only some years later a suggestion was made that they might be given cabbage.) It could not last and the separation occurred after a year although friendship remained between this ill-assorted pair.

Much of the later part of Mary's life was spent in visiting India and campaigning for women's education there, although her uncompromising nature and carelessness of the need for tact gained as many enemies as friends for this cause. However she gained a serene conviction in her later years that she had sown the seed of reform: generations to come would carry on her tremendous work.

By now Mary had become internationally famous. She was invited to travel throughout Europe, America and Canada, to attend conferences and give lectures. Her opinions were invited and respected by all persons of influence, including politicians, reformers, Florence Nightingale, Charles Dickens and even Princess Alice, second daughter of Queen Victoria, who was much involved in charitable works in the newly federated state of Germany. Princess Alice wrote admiringly to her mother: "Only think, old Miss Carpenter spoke on all subjects relating to women's work in England... her great experience has been of value to us all." Queen Victoria responded by inviting Mary for a private interview at Windsor castle, for which Mary set aside the frugal habits of a lifetime and bought herself an elegant claret silk dress, and white gloves. The encounter was a great success, and Mary later wrote a word for word account of it.

The last year of Mary's life she had her adopted daughter, Roseanna with her. She was there for the final evening when Mary, indefatigable as ever, had written to an old American friend, W.L.Garrison (an ex-slave and leading anti-slavery campaigner), whom at Mary's invitation had often moved her pupils with his accounts of the hardships of slavery that were even greater than their own . She invited him to stay, when she proposed to have "about a hundred friends to tea in Red Lodge drawing-room." By ten o'clock the letter was finished and her good-night to Roseanna said. The next morning she was found dead in her bed, a peaceful end to a most extraordinary career. She was buried with her beloved father, Lant Carpenter, in Arnos Vale Cemetery.

Following Mary's death in 1877 a committee, answerable to trustees, managed the Red Lodge school. One of the trustees was Elizabeth Sturge, who is described in greater detail later in this chapter. The Minute Books indicated that the majority of girls placed out on licence did well, with a minority absconding or being returned to the school. Punishments within the school were relatively few: separation from others on a diet of bread and water appeared to be the most extreme. In 1880 Miss Sturge discussed the medical supervision of the girls with Dr Walker Dunbar (see Chapter 3) who was subsequently appointed Honorary Medical Attendant to the school.

SACRED TO THE MEMORY OF
MARY CARPENTER

Mary Carpenter's plaque in Bristol Cathedral

Mary would surely have been pleased that it was James Martineau who composed the inscription for the memorial plaque in Bristol Cathedral:

"Sacred to the memory of Mary Carpenter, foremost among the founders of Reformatory and Industrial Schools in this city and realm. Neither the claims of private duty, nor the tastes of a cultured mind, could withdraw her compassionate eye from the uncared for children of the streets. Loving them while yet unlovely, she so formed them to the fair and good as to inspire others with her faith and hope, and thus led the way to a national system of moral rescue and preventive discipline... Desiring to extend her work of piety and love, many who honoured her have instituted in her name some homes for the homeless young, and now complete their tribute of affection by erecting this memorial."

Frances Cobbe (1822 - 1904)

Frances Cobbe crossing the Avon Gorge with her brothes, suspended in a wicker cradle

The adventurous Frances Power Cobbe could not have been more different from sober Mary Carpenter, and the story of their association is a tragi-comic one.

Frances was the only daughter of an expansive and easy-going Irish landowner. After a childhood running wild at home in Newbridge, near Dublin, with her four brothers and up to thirty young relations who came to stay in the holidays, her parents sent her to a boarding-school in Brighton at the age of thirteen. It was a desperate measure on their part to have their daughter attain a few lady-like accomplishments. One of her brothers accompanied her, with a visit to Clifton en route. It was 1836, and the foundation-stone for the Suspension Bridge had just been laid. An iron bar spanned the Avon Gorge and, after a judicious tip to the workmen, Frances made the adventurous crossing of the Gorge suspended in a cradle. It is, perhaps, not surprising that this intrepid Irish girl hated the two years spent at school in Brighton! Subsequently she read widely and studied Greek and geometry with a tutor. Once home, she took over responsibility for the housekeeping from her ailing mother, who had already been lamed in an earlier accident. She died when Frances was twenty-four.

This was a time of much controversy in the Anglican Church. During the 1830's widespread distress and actual starvation affected the people of England, and in 1845 a potato blight heralded the famine in Ireland, year after year destroying the staple food of almost the entire peasant population. For some, atheism and radicalism was the answer to the terrible social injustice that aggravated such disasters. For others, as for Frances, the social conflict of the times led to a questioning of religious belief.

Frances struggled to accept orthodox Christianity and by the age of twenty, called herself an agnostic.Further reading led her to embrace 'Theism' (a belief similar to Unitarianism). She became one of a group of influential young writers who included Harriet Martineau, the Irish Protestant John Tyndall, A.H.Clough, George Eliot and Charles Darwin. She confessed her religious 'heresy' to her father after her mother's death. The result was banishment to her brother's farm in beautiful but wild Donegal.

A year later she was summoned home. Much needed to be done to relieve the victims of the famine on her father's estate, and this may have united father and daughter again. During this time she started her first book, although she complained "How was I to find a quiet hour to compose it? Like most women I was bound hand and foot by a fine web of little duties and attentions, which men never feel or brush aside remorselessly..."

Nevertheless she wrote a number of books and articles, supporting women's suffrage and legislation relating to the rights of women within marriage. Later in life she wrote the *Claims of Brutes*, having become an ardent anti-vivisectionist.

After her father's death in 1857 she inherited a generous personal income and spent nearly a year travelling widely in Europe and the Middle East - equivalent to the Grand Tour undertaken by many wealthy young men at that time. But after this taste of freedom she needed an occupation as well as the loving companionship and the understanding that she had only lately achieved with her father.

A mutual friend, Lady Byron, suggested she should go to be an assistant to Mary Carpenter. She set off for Bristol with high, romantic hopes, of which she wrote subsequently:

> *My special attraction to Miss Carpenter was the belief that I should find her at once a very religious woman, and one so completely*

outside the pale of orthodoxy that I should be sure to meet from her the sympathy I had never yet been privileged to enjoy; and at all events be able to assist her labours with freedom of conscience.

Susanna Winkworth described Frances at about this time: "she is a most cheering person, so fresh and genuine, sparkling on the surface with geniality, fun and affection and at the same time deep both in character and in intellect as very few are..." In appearance she was "fair, fat ...quick, frank, jolly manners". Her good nature was about to become most severely tested.

The two women could hardly have been more different. Although Mary welcomed the help that Frances was offering, she had little personal need of further emotional support, and was completely unperturbed, let alone unmoved, by Frances' hearty desires for physical and emotional companionship. Mary was obsessed by her work for the deprived street children of Bristol, with no time to spare for even a square meal, let alone other matters.

To begin with Frances made a great effort to fit in with Mary Carpenter's regime. The street boys attending the Ragged Schools called "Cobweb" after her. "I'm tougher than a cobweb", she retorted. "And fatter too" was their response. Although she could laugh at the boys she had to struggle with the work in the schools and in the Reformatory, repelled by the dirty and often diseased children, and, unlike Mary, with no experience of teaching.

Sadly, Frances realised that all Mary's attention and love was for her work. She later wrote of her friend with resigned affection:

> *The prevailing characteristic of Mary Carpenter ... was a high and strong resolution which made her whole path much like that of a plough in a well-drawn furrow, which goes straight on in its own beneficent way, and gently pushes aside into little ridges all intervening people and things.*

When Frances finally accepted the inevitable and left Red Lodge House in December 1859, her "health broken down", she went to live at Belgrave House, Durdham Down. For a while after her recovery she continued to work at Red Lodge and the Ragged Schools, and slowly began to find a new purpose. Frances had come to know the daughter of the late Dean of Bristol, who had taught the Red Lodge girls for many years. Increasingly she became involved with Miss Elliot's work for sick and infirm paupers, having a particular sympathy for the incurable poor. She visited the Workhouses and gave support to the friendless girls, whose fate was to be sent untrained and without protection into service at the age of sixteen, for which they were paid a pittance and from which there was little escape: another form of slavery in all but name. It is of interest that Liverpool and Bristol, the two cities that gained most from the slave trade, employed more servants per head of population than any other city in England!

Doubtless some girls were treated kindly but many were grossly exploited, with prostitution as their only way out. Miss Elliot and her sister ran a Sunday afternoon school for these girls, which Frances described as very successful in attracting girls with no other ways of attaining any education.

About this time, Frances and Miss Elliot collaborated on the publication, Housing of the Poor in Large Cities. In the 1860's Frances, once more in advance of women of the time, became a journalist in London contributing to several newspapers. For the next twenty years she wrote and lectured, supporting the rights of women, whether for votes or in marriage. She acquired a wide circle of intellectual friends, both men and women, becoming well known for her wide interests and for her luncheon parties consisting of many courses. She became grossly fat and suffered from gout but remained jolly throughout. It was during this time that she met Mary Lloyd, an aspiring sculptress, who responded to her need for love and companionship. They set up home together, with a family of pet dogs, moving to Wales in 1884. It was here that this early feminist eventually died in 1904 after a courageous and unconventional life.

The Sturge Sisters

The Quaker Sturges

Elizabeth Sturge (1850 - 1944)

Elizabeth was born in 1850, the third of six sisters and three brothers of a Quaker family in Bristol. The lives of the Sturges were interwoven into the close Bristol community of middle-class educationalists, philanthropists, political and social reformers of their time; they knew them all, and everyone knew the Sturges. Between them they had a tremendous impact on education, housing and political reform in Bristol. The lives of the Sturges are a good illustration of how, in the days before country-wide legislation to support and educate the poor, much pioneering work was due to the efforts of unmarried women with private means, who nevertheless were called on to drop all work commitments when their families needed them as nurses or companions of aged relatives.

Money must have been short as the girls were sent away to be educated in turns, but the girls' schooling was supplemented by attending the new 'lectures for ladies' that were subsequently held at University College. Elizabeth seems to have been the first of the sisters to find regular work. She taught in the Friends' Sunday school and had been visitor and manager of one or two girls' schools. With their non-conformist background in common, Elizabeth knew Mary Carpenter very well, and was slowly drawn into her sphere of work. Despite having little experience of the type of girls given shelter by Mary, she helped to supervise the Red Lodge School with two of her sisters, and eventually took over its administration. Then she stood in for the Matron while she took what must have been a much-needed holiday:

> *"It was the most strenuous fortnight I ever spent. Some of the girls were of violent and ungovernable temper, and at times there were distressing scenes... one had to be able to act firmly and quickly to prevent the spread of disorder."*

There was to be little respite from such strenuous undertakings. When Mary Carpenter died suddenly in 1877, no-one had been designated to take over the running of the School. A Body of Managers was hastily organised, and Elizabeth Sturge was invited to join them. Shortly afterwards she became Honorary Secretary, and then for the next five years ran the school with the help of the Managers.

By 1883 Elizabeth was able to give up her work at the Red Lodge and help her sister Emily with School Board work. The next few years were spent in helping various members of her family in old age, bereavement or illness after childbirth. Then, by chance, she heard that the housing reformer, Octavia Hill, needed a helper in London - unpaid, naturally. Elizabeth had been left a small annual income with which to support herself, and allied herself with Octavia Hill, being trained in the renovation and management of working class dwellings, which Octavia was reclaiming from the Bristol slums and resettling with the 'respectable' poor.

Elizabeth was soon running her own district of Southwark, and joined her sisters Carta and Caroline who were living in Bloomsbury. But her mother's death in 1891 forced her to return as a 'home daughter' to support her father and sister Helen. The sisters were to live together until Elizabeth's death in 1944.

Elizabeth's experience of housing in Southwark was to prove very useful after the eventual death of her father. Although by the turn of the century new housing was beginning to replace the slums, it was only a marginal improvement. Then premises were bought in Barton Hill to form part of the University Settlement, "for the systematic study of the social and industrial conditions, and for the promotion of the general neighbourhood." Elizabeth assessed the repairs required in a row of cottages, and supervised the work until completion.

In 1907 she and Dr. Eliza Walker Dunbar (see chapter 3) joined together to provide a Garden Suburb in Bristol. Other cities had already planned and built such suburbs, providing low-cost housing in pleasant surroundings. Elizabeth and Eliza knew, from their different professional perspectives, that much of the illness affecting the poor could be prevented by providing houses with the extra space and fresh air of a garden. If only subsequent national housing policies had been allowed the financial flexibility to follow suit!

The women found a suitable 26 acre plot near the station in Shirehampton, on which fourteen houses could be built per acre. A committee was formed, and advertisements were placed in the papers for shares in the enterprise - which was to recoup its financial outlay from rents. Supporters of the scheme included the Quaker Fry and Pease families, Elizabeth's sister, Helen, and other members of the extended Sturge clan. Initially, rents were set at between six and ten shillings a week, and they remained at this level until 1918.

'Ideal' housing designed in 1907 for working families at the Bristol Garden Suburb

The prospectus shows the plans of the two and three bedroom houses. All have a WC next to the back door, entered from the outside, but only a few had bathrooms. Although the rents were actually too high for the very poor, there are only occasional reports of the houses being re-let. This was because demand for housing was increasing to what was an 'abnormal' level by 1918, as all new house building had ceased in 1916. After the end of World War 1, army allowances were increasingly able to cover the rents and must have contributed to the stability of the tenancies.

Five years later, in 1923, the Garden Suburb Company was taken over by the Bristol Housing Company. The capital left over was transferred to the Bristol Church tenants Association for the rehabilitation of housing and tenants. So the very poor - if they were church-goers - may have got the help they needed at last!

Apart from her work with social housing, Elizabeth was also involved with Redland High School, when she joined the school council in 1896. She was much valued for her experience and advice, and on her retirement in 1917 she was appointed vice-president in recognition of her services. In the school's jubilee year, in 1932 she was still able to write a short history of the school at the age of 82. Her further contribution to women's education came through her friendship with Canon John Gamble, the vicar of St. Mary the Virgin at Leigh Woods. Through her influence the Canon left much of his wealth to promote the higher education of women. As Bristol University was already co-educational, it was deemed ineligible to benefit from the will, and instead the new colleges for women at Oxford and Cambridge each received £5000, while the Upper School of Redland received £21,000 towards new buildings and scholarships.

Elizabeth ended a long and fulfilling life in 1944, aged 94, lovingly cared for by her sister Helen, who died the following year.

Helen Sturge (c.1858 - 1945)

Helen was described as being the 'home daughter', which at the time was a career in itself, and the lot of many Victorian spinsters. Helen immersed herself in the new intellectual opportunities for women in Bristol by attending lectures in French, Geology and literature and continuing her studies at the University College. She added a course on Egyptology and Oriental languages to her accomplishments, in preparation for a solo trip to Cairo and up the Nile with a Cook's Tour. In 1905 she took her sister Elizabeth with her on a second trip to the Sudan.

Life in the Sturge household was a busy one: visiting lecturers were invited to stay, nephews, nieces and cousins were often around during termtime, especially; two nieces attended Clifton High School as day girls. Helen helped her sister Emily's activities in the Liberal Association, becoming the Secretary of the Association. She was also involved in local welfare work with the shop and factory girls at the Preventative Mission, and took over the post of Superintendent of the Girls' side of the Friends' Sunday Schools.

After the death of their father, Elizabeth and Helen left their house in Tyndalls Park and moved to a smaller house, devoting themselves to the struggle for the female vote; the third generation of Sturges to do so. In 1840 their great-aunt Ada Knight had campaigned for votes for women, followed, after an initial period of disapproval, by their mother Charlotte. Helen Sturge had worked among the shop and factory girls at the Preventative Mission, and as Secretary to the Bristol Women's Liberal Association. Helen died in 1945.

Emily Sturge (1842 - 1883)

Elizabeth's sister Emily had broken new ground when she had been appointed a member of the School Council of Redland High School; her life is described in greater detail in Chapter 2. After Emily's unexpected early death, Elizabeth was appointed in her place and soon made her mark in her own right. She joined her sister Helen as a 'Home Daughter', looking after their father and the two nieces from London who attended Clifton High School.

Mary Charlotte Sturge (1852 - 1929)

Mary, known as Carta, was the fourth Sturge daughter, and had a reputation as being the most academic in spite of her reputation of being a "madcap" at school - which may say something about the quality of education there. Nevertheless she taught successfully at the Friends' Sunday School, assisted her old school at Weston super Mare and became a governess for a short while. She soon realised her lack of qualifications and enrolled at the Bristol University College to study for the Cambridge Higher Local examination, which she passed after three years. With this success, and a glowing testimonial from Mrs. Mary Paley Marshall, (lecturer in Political Economy) she studied Moral Sciences at Newnham College, Cambridge and passed with second class honours in 1887, although she was one of the many women who were not awarded their degree until 1923. Carta went on to lecture in moral philosophy at London University and around the country.

Caroline Sturge (1861 - 1922)

Caroline Sturge, M.D.
1861—1922

The youngest of the sisters was Caroline, born in 1861. She also attended lectures at the new University College in Bristol after having been kept at home by her mother to attend a local day school. Caroline was inspired to become a doctor by her sister in law, Dr Emily Bovell, and her cousin, Dr Ann Clark, who were members of a group of pioneering medical students at Edinburgh, despite the hosility of male students who threw rotten eggs at the girls on their way to Anatomy class. Debarred from clinical training, the women went to London where the leader of their group, Miss Jex-Blake, set up her own medical school for women. In due course, the Royal Free Hospital allowed the women to attend there for clinical teaching. As they were still unable to obtain a medical degree in Britain, Ann Clark and Emily Bovell studied abroad. Ann took advantage of the regulations and re-sat her finals in Dublin in order to obtain registration as an M.R.C.P. in Britain, and went on to practice in Birmingham. Emily completed her studies in Paris where she met Will Sturge, himself recently qualified. The couple practiced in London, where Emily took over abdominal surgery at the Elizabeth Garrett Anderson hospital from Frances Hoggan, who had studied in Zurich with Eliza Dunbar.

Despite the example of these pioneering yet highly respectable family relations and friends, Caroline's parents refused consent for her to leave home to study medicine. In 1883 fortune favoured her, in the form of an annuity from an old uncle. Her ambition could not be pursued in Bristol at the time, and Edinburgh remained implacably hostile. Caroline studied at University College, Bristol, to obtain the qualifications which would allow her to enter medical school in London. With no further objection from her father, Caroline started medical training at the age of 23, in 1884, at the London School of Medicine founded by Miss Jex-Blake. When she finally qualified, Caroline specialised in midwifery, becoming a consultant at the Elizabeth Garrett Anderson Hospital in 1894. Caroline retired early in order to look after an adopted aunt of the family. She lived with her in Winscombe, Somerset, and kept up her professional interests by working with the District nursing Society, the Committees of the County Institutions for mentally handicapped children, as an examiner for the Central Midwives' Board. She died in 1922, of an incurable brain tumour.

Susanna Winkworth (1820 -1884)

The Winkworth sisters, Susanna and Catherine, had been born into an intensely evangelical household in London. Susanna later wrote:

"While still quite children we were sometimes taken to three services on Sunday, besides teaching in Sunday-school (before the age of twelve); and a missionary meeting at Exeter Hall was the greatest delight of our lives".

Novels and fairy-tales were prohibited, as were most "story-books" - and we can guess at the pietistic nature of those that were permitted. But, in Susanna's words, an "unlimited range of pasture in travels and history" was available, and the children created their own fairy-land, peopled by sprites, and their own "kingdoms" of Natural History. We are reminded of the Bronte children although their imaginings reached wilder heights than those of the Winkworths.

The girls' father was a silk merchant who later moved his family to Manchester, where the family became used to social work among the poor and had even assisted Mrs Gaskell there, the newly famous biographer of Charlotte Bronte. In 1864 Susanna and Catherine Winkworth moved to Bristol. Once settled in Clifton, (there is now a plaque at 31 Cornwallis Crescent), Susanna undertook district visiting, especially in Hotwells, "the poor district of Clifton". Here the houses were "mostly large and let out in tenements, and the noise and dirt made by children coming in and out caused their rejection from any but the poorest and worse-kept..." Unlike Mary Carpenter, who worked with the outcasts of society, Susanna was struck by the needs of "decent poor people with large families". She aimed to provide accommodation for them and to improve the neighbourhood at the same time. A contemporary biographer wrote:

> *She took several houses in Dowry Square, which were at that time inhabited by a very rough and low set of people, put them into a thorough state of repair at a great expense, and placed in each a superintendent to let the rooms, collect the rents, and enforce order in the house. The cellars were turned into wash-houses, coal-cellars provided to obviate the necessity for coals being kept in cupboards in the rooms, and a set of rules framed to prevent the interference of one tenant with the comfort of others. The advantages of these abodes were soon recognised by the respectable families in the neighbourhood, and the whole character of the Square was raised ...*

The rents were too low for an economic return, and it was found that the roofs of three of the houses had to be rebuilt; in addition there were problems of management. Nevertheless Susanna gained much experience in these pioneer efforts to improve the housing of the poor.

In 1872 she also undertook the management of a Sanitary Mission. A woman was engaged to visit the homes of the poor to show them how to use disinfectants, to teach them habits of cleanliness, and to collect small sums for the purchase of sheets, which were supplied at wholesale prices. Susanna collected the money to carry out this work, superintended it and wrote pamphlets and lectures on Sanitation.

In 1874 Susanna discovered a plot of land for sale suitable for building 'model dwellings'. She studied blocks of model houses in London, prepared plans and enlisted the support of the principal business men in Bristol. A company was formed for the purpose, including members of

Susanna Winkworth's "model dwellings" on Jacob's Wells Rd, very run down by 1957. This photograph was taken shortly prior to demolition.

families such as the Frys and the Wills. The land was purchased on which were erected the Jacob's Wells Buildings, which were demolished in the 1960's. These dwellings, built for £20,000 and designed in a Scots Baronial style, were revolutionary. Each low-rent flat had water, gas and a balcony, and the result was a very low incidence of infectious diseases. Subsequently the Brandon Buildings were built on an adjoining piece of land.

Susanna followed the methods of Octavia Hill in having the rents collected by ladies who could advise and befriend the tenants. This provision of housing for the poor was successful socially, although less so financially.

Susanna died in November 1884 aged sixty-four, and was commemorated by the naming of Winkworth Place in St Paul's, Bristol.

Emma Saunders (1841-1927)

Few names from the army of women who were devoted to good works survive in Bristol's records, but one of them, Emma Saunders, has a permanent white marble memorial in the form of a plaque outside Temple Meads railway station. Emma Saunders was known as "The railway men's Friend". She lived in Sion Hill, Clifton, and devoted fifty years of her life to improving the lot of railway men and their families.

When the Clifton extension Severn tunnel was being built in 1878, Emma set up Sunday religious services and bible classes in a branch of the Railway Mission there, followed by Monday Mothers' meetings. She was anxious to provide spiritual as well as material help to the workers, whose lives of danger and drudgery were often made bearable through frequent recourse to the taverns after work. She began visiting the rail-waymen wherever they were to be found. She would visit six stations along the Clifton line in one afternoon, and nobody would be missed out, either on the current or following shift: clerks, inspectors, drivers, firemen, porters, shunters, plate-layers, carboys, refreshment staff and cleaners. She walked to the engine sheds, repairing sheds, coaling sheds, carting depots, goods yards, tarpaulin sheds, waterside cranes, and harbour railways, distributing her own, monthly, hand-printed Bible texts, together with 2,000 copies of the Railway Messenger, which carried her selected Bible text on the cover. Inside were details of further religious meetings. Each man would also receive a little gift from a bag tied around her waist which left her arms free: a flower picked from her Sion Hill garden, seaweed (presumably to remind him of all-too rare excursions to the coast five miles away), shells or a lavender bag. Whatever the men made of these gifts, she was held in tremendous affection: her help was kindly and practical as well.

Emma Saunders' plaque at Temple Meads Railway Station

Emma visited those at home who had been arrested for drunkenness or other clashes with the law, and suspended from work. She financed a bowls team to keep the men from the temptation of drink in their spare time. Emma even provided an annual tea and once paid for a young man's set of false teeth to enjoy it with! She was concerned, too, about the horses that were used to haul railway freight from the station, and gave each of the railway carters a copy of Anna Sewell's *'Black Beauty'*, which had been published in 1877 to tremendous public acclaim and concern.

Out of her work developed the Railway Workers Institute at 66 Mead St, later at 4-6 Bath Rd where workers could hold meetings, and enjoy meals and games of billiards, bagatelle or skittles away from the temptations of public houses. Even on Christmas Day Emma visited the Institute to distribute mince pies to those who had to be on duty.

On her 80th birthday, 5,000 workers of the GWR and MR railways contributed to present her with gifts of furniture and an Illustrated Address, and named the Emma Saunders bed in the Railway Home at Dawlish in Devon. When she died, her little coffin was carried on the shoulders of four high-ranking uniformed men along the streets from her home to Christchurch, and it was followed by an army of railway men of all grades, from inspectors to young porters, each with a daffodil button-hole in memory of the gifts of their old friend.

Ada Vachell (1866 - 1924)

Ada Vachell's 1924 funeral was equally impressive: *"Seldom if ever can the great mother church of the city of Bristol have presented a more impressive and touching sight than yesterday afternoon, when for nearly an hour a seemingly endless stream of cripples poured through the great north door to pay their last tribute of respect to their beloved Sister Ada"* wrote the reporter of the Bristol Evening paper.

Provision for the handicapped in late Victorian Bristol was patchy. A Blind Asylum had been started by the Quakers in Callow Hill St. in 1793. It only closed in 1967, at a time when children and helpers were integrated into mainstream education. A School for the Deaf had opened in Bristol by 1843, in Park Row, much later than many others throughout the country - Edinburgh had one already in 1760. But for those otherwise physically handicapped, especially for children, there was little provision.

As uneducated and helpless adults the prospects of earning an independent living were difficult, and until as late as 1930 the terror of the workhouse still loomed over those unable to support themselves. It was to this neglected and even shunned section of society that Ada devoted her life: the Guild that she founded in Bristol catered for all handicaps without segregation and with many advantages in the way of mutual help, especially on holidays. Thousands of disadvantaged young people found new life and hope thanks to this devoted and visionary woman.

Ada was born in Cardiff, in 1866 ,where her father was a well-known businessman from a Quaker family and thrice Mayor of the city. Ada and her two siblings developed scarlet fever: the two died and Ada survived but with bilateral deafness that increased during her lifetime. After this catastrophe her father became increasingly prone to depression, and in 1875 her parents left the ill-fated City of Cardiff for her mother's birthplace, Bristol. Here Ada and her new baby brother grew up in a spacious home and garden, Severn House, Sneyd Park.

A cheerful collection of 'Poor Things' outside Bragg's Lane

Ada left school early to be with her beloved mother whose health was deteriorating, and who died when Ada was in her twenties. Despite or possibly because of her lack of formal education, Ada was avid to experience as much as possible; and her energetic nature shunned the conventional social round. She went to university lectures, played chess, went on walking tours and even lived in a fisherman's cottage for a few days, and slept in the open, just to see what it would feel like. She was insatiably curious about other people's lives, and once spent a day in London selling flowers - she said her hollow cough helped sales!

Her early family losses and her deafness must have channelled Ada's enthusiastic and individualistic temperament into care for others. Already in her late teens she would invite young servants and errand boys to the kitchen or to her sitting-room on Sunday afternoons and evenings; she later developed this into a 'clubroom' for factory girls. In a forerunner of future activities, she took the errand boys for a trip to Clevedon. This escapade turned into a tragi-comedy with the pony trap driver drunk by the time of return: with great calmness Ada stood up behind him for miles, successfully directing his driving all the way home. She took to what her parents called 'slumming', visiting poor homes and seeking out the sick and afflicted, and giving practical help. She started a Sunday class for servants living nearby and it was they who started calling her Sister Ada, as a joke. The name stuck.

Ada's early work with young people developed into the provision of a club for girls in the city which included visits to her home and garden, and, inevitably, to picnics and outings in the countryside. At this time she pioneered the idea of country holidays in which she and other workers shared. There was nothing patronising about Ada who enjoyed all the activities she set up for her club members, and through her visits to families in Bristol she had developed a greater understanding of the girls' life and customs.

Ada's real life's work began when she was taken to see the unfortunately titled **Guild Of Poor Things** in London; this was a home for crippled and handicapped children, started in 1895, and Ada determined to open the same kind of operation in Bristol, which she eventually did in 1895. The **Guild of The Brave Poor Things** - mercifully renamed the **Guild of the Handicapped** - acquired its own purpose-built headquarters in Bragg's Lane, St. Philips, where the building still stands. Ada's simple but effective idea was to give the disabled and handicapped access to music, literature and art, and to the pleasures of the countryside, and to help them in practical ways, with mobility aids, clothing, exercise, and holidays. The idea had come from Mrs Ewing's book *'The Story of a Short Life'* (a tale of a boy crippled by an accident and thus unable to be a soldier). The Guild developed into an almost militaristic order with flags and badges and the motto *'Laetus sorte mea'*, (happy is my lot). As in the story the courage of soldiers was to be demanded of the handicapped together with the ideal of soldiers for Christ. The sentiments seem alien to many of us to-day, but the comradeship and activities were for many the only alleviation of a life characterised by poverty and loneliness.

A few years later, in 1899, she initiated the Invalid Children's School with the assistance of her friend, the Rev. Urijah Thomas, Chairman of the Bristol School Board. The Board provided a teacher, furnished room and equipment, with a voluntary committee to raise funds for the transport of the children and the provision of a school nurse. At that time it was far-sighted to have a school-leaving age of 16 for the children (instead of 14) thus enabling craft and hand-work to be taught in the latter years.

St. Peter's Hospital, the first Bristol workhouse established in 1698, formerly the Old Mint

To find those most in need of assistance Ada would spend day after day tramping the slum alleys, often sped on her way by the advice of the relieving officers (who provided a modicum on which to live for those unable to work). She describes how she would frequently take flowers with her to break the barriers of suspicion, but usually found acceptance. Indeed her interest would often stimulate interest from the carers of the unfortunate individual who was often ignored and found in a corner or lying on a bed.

For many years the Guild met in a Settlement in Broad Plain. Ada started regular meetings for all and developed clubs for boys and girls, activities for children, a library and clothing club and music, especially appreciated by the blind. Organised lectures were very popular with the men who were often starved of intellectual stimulation. (Alas! no lectures for the women, although Ada was a supporter of women's suffrage).

By 1910 the Guild needed new accommodation and for this dream Ada needed five thousand pounds. The money came, and architects drew up plans for the site, trustees were found and the 'Guild Heritage' building arose: a large hall, club rooms, gymnasium, class-rooms. The dream had come true, although with it a greater load of work and responsibility.

For one woman with her helpers this might have been enough. But the countryside had continued to beckon. Increasing numbers of Guild members were sent away for a week, at first boarded out in cottages and later in a rented farm. But a home of their own was needed and at last in about 1906 the Churchill Home was provided by friends giving adequate accommodation and three acres of land. Children and adults came all the year round: for many children the first time they had seen flowers and trees growing in the country. The delicate ones thrived and became tanned away from the sunless gloom of their slum dwellings: care was given for those with hip disease or tuberculosis of the bone who needed months of rest and fresh air. One tragic man had been forced by extreme poverty to enter the dreaded workhouse but had two weeks away in the Home to set against the misery of his existence - misery bravely borne.

'Sister' Ada endlessly raised funds, to set up an apprenticeship scheme to help them find work, and provide them with tools, a work suit of clothes, and funds to start a business; she also formed a Scout troupe and set up a holiday home at Churchill. When in 1921 the lease on the home ran out it was offered to her at a very low price. With the endorsement of the Lord Mayor of Bristol she launched a public appeal in the teeth of the post war depression; hundreds of pounds poured in, and the Home was secured. A later appeal for £5,000 to provide a Guild House in Bristol was also successful: the new headquarters had club rooms, classroom, a gymnasium, and a small shop selling the handi-crafts of the Guild members.

She died shortly after this last tremendous achievement in 1924, having lived the last fourteen years of her life in Foley Cottage on Hampton Rd, next to the Quaker Meeting House. An inscription in a corner of the memorial to Ada on the wall of the Cathedral commemorates her with the crossed sword and crutch as the icon of the Guild:

TO KEEP IN MEMORY

ADA VACHELL

FOUNDER OF THE BRISTOL GUILD OF THE HANDICAPPED

A WOMAN MADE STRONG BY GOD
TO GIVE
LOVE TO THE LONELY
VALOUR TO THE WEAK
COMFORT TO THE SORROWFUL

MCMXXIII

2   The Educators

The status of women in Bristol, as everywhere else, always depended greatly on the way they were educated. Until elementary education became compulsory in 1870, girls would be educated at the whim of their parents. The very poor might attend a ragged school to be educated purely for a life in service. Working class girls might go to a dame school, or a church school for a few years at the cost of a few pennies a week, and most middle class girls would be sketchily educated by their mothers or by governesses at home, or at one of the numerous private "academies" that the city boasted. Lucky ones, like Hannah More, received a serious classical education.

Hannah More (1745 - 1833)

Hannah More's life not only spans two centuries but in many ways it typifies the changing public attitudes to the public role of women in the eighteenth and nineteenth centuries. In this chapter we examine her huge contribution to female education and philanthropy in Bristol, but Hannah was also a controversial patron of the arts and a tremendously successful playwright, as we shall see in Chapters 4 and 5.

Her life started quietly and happily in the school-house in Fishponds where her father Jacob had been appointed school-master by his patron,

Norbonne Berkeley. Jacob married Mary Grace, a farmer's daughter, and Hannah was the fourth of five daughters who were to spend most of their lives together.

Hannah was a precocious child, taught to read by her mother from the age of three, and at an early age scribbling verses and stories. Both parents were unusual in that they encouraged their daughters to learn more than the three Rs and domestic skills. Hannah was taught Latin and mathematics by her father, and French by her eldest sister, Mary, who attended a French school in Bristol. What was even more unusual was that at the age of nineteen, Mary, with the assistance of her younger sister, Betty, opened a school for girls in Trinity Street, Bristol, moving to Park Street four years later. The sisters ran their school for over thirty years from 1758 to 1790. The younger girls joined them for an initial period as pupils, then pupil-teachers and later as assistants. During this time they took advantage of public lectures to broaden their education.

It was not surprising that the school opened by the More sisters in Park Street in 1758 soon earned the reputation of being the best school for girls in the entire West Country. There appeared the following announcement in a Bristol newspaper:

> *On Monday after Easter will be opened a school for young ladies by Mary More and sisters, where will be carefully taught French, Reading, Writing, Arithmetic and needlework. A dancing master will attend.*

The school was first at 6, Trinity Street and four years later moved to the fashionable address of 43, Park Street. Mary was Principal of the school aged 19 and sister Betty, 17, was the housekeeper. Sisters Sally, Hannah and Patty started as pupils, then became under-governesses and finally teachers. Friends raised the start-up costs by subscription and many local wealthy families were patrons. The school remained under the care of the More sisters - " All women of admirable sense and unaffected behaviour" according to Mrs. Elizabeth Montagu, a lady of London High Society, until 1790, and the school took as many as 60 pupils at a time, a very high figure at a time when an academy could consist of only half a dozen.

The girls were carefully chaperoned - though one, Clementina Clarke, was famously abducted - and their education a liberal one: Hannah More would take school parties to see plays at the Theatres Royal in Bristol and Bath, and in 1773 she wrote an edifying yet extraordinarily successful play, *A Search After Happiness*, for them to perform, as well as nursery rhymes, moral tales and versions of bible stories. (A Search after Happiness was still being regularly performed in the Theatres Royal of

Bristol and Bath 42 years later.) Qualified masters came in to teach the girls Italian, Spanish and Latin. Fees, including tuition, board, dancing and music, were £20 per annum.

This was an exceptionally good education for girls; the seminaries and academies that flourished in 18th century Bristol were concerned mainly with giving girls that kind of accomplishments that made them marriageable. They learned dancing and drawing, they sang, they practised the art of conversation - and were barely literate. As Sheridan's Mrs. Malaprop says in *A School For Scandal*:

> *I don't think so much learning becomes a young woman... I would send her at nine years old, to a boarding school in order to learn a little ingenuity and artifice.*

In the teeth of popular nervousness at the growing emphasis on educating women, Hannah More was becoming such an acknowledged expert on the subject of education for females that she was consulted on the education of George IV's daughter, Princess Charlotte, and subsequently devised a daunting regime to give the poor girl a rigorous intellectual training.

By now Hannah was mixing in artistic and aristocratic circles on her visits to London. She had been introduced to women known as the Bluestockings, which included Dr Johnson's friend and biographer Mrs Thrale and Fanny Burney. Here she was acknowledged as a poet and became a welcome addition to their intellectual circle. However London did not have a monopoly of thinkers and artists. Hannah's family knew that of Thomas Chatterton, the boy poet who gained posthumous fame after his suicide in London. She also met the philosopher, David Hume, as well as other men and women of note in Bristol.

At this time the Evangelical movement was also gaining strength. John Wesley's New Room, the Methodist meeting house in Bristol had been opened in 1739. The chapel, with rooms above, where he stayed, still stands as an oasis of relative peace in the middle of Broadmead shopping centre. Hannah's next-door neighbour in Park Street was Dr Stonehouse, an Evangelical who influenced her religious development. He had taken a great interest in her since he first knew her as an intelligent, lively girl: he had arranged that Mr Turner, who had jilted Hannah, should settle an annuity of £200 on her, and it was he who had introduced her to the actor David Garrick, and his wife Eva. From this it was clear that he was not averse to the theatre, although he maintained a watchful eye on Hannah's activities in London and made sure that she would keep Sundays free from frivolity. With Garrick's death in 1779, Hannah lost her love for London gaiety, and although she continued to visit London annually, staying with Eva Garrick and meeting old and new friends, her energies were being channelled more directly into education. Hannah questioned the narrow prevailing philosophy of education for girls in her book *Strictures on Female Education*, written in 1779, but it would be a mistake to see her as a feminist. She maintained that the point of educating girls was to fit them for "the practical purposes of life" - by which she did not mean careers other than the traditional path of marriage and motherhood.

In these feminine roles, Hannah claimed, girls could aspire to the highest calling possible in life by influencing public morale and re-awakening the spirit of religion, provided they were given the right kind of education. She attacked the "phrenzy of accomplishments" thrust on most girls, which gave them no time to read, or think clearly, and while producing young women who were "flirtatious, vain and over-tired." The right way for a girl was:

> *...the kind of study that will lead her to be intent on the realities - will give precision to her ideas - will make an exact mind. She should cultivate every kind of study, which instead of stimulating her sensibility, will chastise it - which will neither create an excessive and false refinement, which will give her definite notions - will bring the imagination under dominion - will lead her to think, to compare and combine, to methodise - which will confer such a power of discrimination that her judgment shall learn to reject what is dazzling, if it be not solid - and prefer not what is striking or bright, or new, but what is just.*

Hannah More's **Strictures on Female Education** contained a solemn chapter on the dangers of an ill-directed sensibility, a topic which Jane Austen was later to deal with more wittily, and humanely, in **'Sense and Sensibility'**. But Hannah More rightly attacked the trivial nature of girls' lives, saying that their education allowed them to indulge their feelings to the exclusion of reason, and made their minds too relaxed by petty pursuits. She complained that men, *"even men of understanding, join in the confederacy against their own happiness by looking for their home companion in the resorts of vanity....if indeed women were mere outside, form and face only, and if mind made up no part in her composition, it could follow that a ballroom was quite as appropriate a place for choosing a wife."*

When the Park Street school was eventually sold in 1789, Hannah's older sisters moved to Bath. Meanwhile she had acquired a cottage at Cowslip Green, near Wrington in Somerset, but it was less idyllic than its name: so damp and cold that the main part of the winter had to be spent in Bath.

Hannah had, perhaps, expected to live most of the year quietly in the country with her devoted sister, Patty. But a new phase in her life started in 1789 following a visit paid by Wilberforce and his sister to Cowslip Green. She had first met him in London at a dinner held to discuss the evils of slavery. Hannah, together with many Evangelicals, was horrified by the cruelties inherent in the slave trade: that trade upon which the prosperity of Bristol rested. She added her voice to those calling for its abolition.

Hannah and Patty urged their visitor to see the splendours of Cheddar Gorge. He returned full of the misery and abject poverty seen in the village. His words have been frequently quoted: *"Miss Hannah More, Something must be done for Cheddar. If you will be at the trouble I will be at the expense."*

Dr. Johnson. friend and mentor to Hannah More

Nowadays with cars and coaches visiting Cheddar Gorge and with easy access to the neighbouring villages it is hard to picture what life was like there two centuries ago. It is even harder to imagine Hannah and Patty visiting these remote and often dangerous areas to alleviate the grinding poverty and to inaugurate a system of schools to tackle the ignorance that accompanied it. They started two types of schools: the Greater Schools were in Cheddar, Shipham and Nailsea, where a teacher was employed to give industrial, agricultural and domestic training to the village children. Two centuries on we may consider it a perpetuation of the rural class system that only farmer's sons were instructed in the three R's for a small fee. But Hannah, like her mentor, Dr Johnson, was a Tory and had no wish to alter the status quo, only to alleviate the associated miseries.

In addition to the Greater Schools, Sunday Schools were held for all children where reading was taught as well as the Scriptures. Adults and adolescents could attend reading classes during the week. As well as the schools, the sisters established Friendly Societies for the women, thus enabling them to have assistance in illness, childbirth or bereavement. A small subscription entitled them to these benefits as well as to religious and domestic instruction.

The Lesser Schools were founded to provide Sunday Schools and evening reading classes. These were held with varying degrees of success at Sandford, Congresbury, Yatton, Chew Magna, Axbridge and even at Wedmore: the latter was 14 miles from Hannah's home. The sisters visited all these areas on foot or on horseback, or sometimes in a farm wagon, undeterred by bad weather or atrocious roads, or indeed by such a mishap such as a fall from a horse. All this in spite of the fact that Hannah suffered from poor health: she had a chronic cough and from a young age had suffered from 'nervous headaches'.

Barley Wood Hannah More's last home

It is difficult to believe that such philanthropic work could arouse hostility. But in fact a battle waged for several years over an initially successful school in Blagdon, set up at the request of the curate, Mr Bere, and a deputation from the parish: a parish notorious for crime. The numbers grew, the crime rate fell and then, surprisingly, Mr Bere started an offensive against the schoolmaster, Mr Yonge. Ostensibly it was fought on aspects of religious doctrine, but it seems likely that Mr Bere found that the power of the pulpit was being threatened by the teaching of the schoolmaster. The details of the battle are complex, involving other clergy, including the Bishop, farmers and local landowners in the neighbourhood. It is ironical that Hannah was even attacked by a high Tory publication, the Anti-Jacobin Review. She came near to complete nervous collapse and eventually closed the school. One wonders whether Hannah's Christianity was proof against a feeling of triumph when Mr Bere in his turn was dismissed by the Rector at the instigation of the

Bishop: perhaps she thankfully accepted the downfall of the curate as an indication of God's will.

In addition to all the visiting and supervising of schools Hannah wrote widely for popular consumption. She had become friendly with the Clapham Sect, a group involved in anti-slavery and evangelicalism which included Macauley, Henry and Marianne Thornton and William Wilberforce. Members of this group, friends and Hannah's sisters were all involved in publishing the Cheap Repository Tracts from 1793 onwards. Several million were sold or distributed at a nominal cost. These were circulated among the poor in their cottages or in the schools, distributed to hospitals, prisons and among the army and navy. Many thousands of Tracts were sent overseas: when Harriet Martineau visited America in 1834 she stated that Hannah More was heard of everywhere: "She was certainly much better known than Shakespeare."

From 1801 the last home of the 'Sisterhood' was at Barley Wood near Wrington: Hannah sold Cowslip Green and her sisters sold the house in Bath. At Barley Wood they received many visitors from all over England and from overseas. Betty, the second eldest, had been nicknamed 'the Wife of the Family' in childhood. It seems sad that her devotion to her sisters may have prevented her from becoming a wife in reality, but perhaps managing this hospitable household was compensation. During this Indian Summer of the sisters Hannah and Patty continued their work among the poor.

Tragically, Hannah's four sisters all died between 1813 and 1819 and she was left alone with her companion, Mary Frowd. In poor health she remained at Barley Wood for another ten years until her final move to the house of Dr Thomas Whalley at 4 Windsor Terrace Clifton, visited by her old friend Wilberforce. Here, in declining health she lived the last few years of her life until she joined her sisters in the graveyard in Wrington where a tablet in the church commemorates her life's work.

Maria Edgeworth
(1768 - 1849)

Hannah More's contemporary Maria Edgeworth, the writer who lived briefly in Princes Buildings, Clifton, shared her views on the poor quality of education for girls. In ***Practical Education***, which she wrote with her father in 1798, Maria claimed that *"it will tend to the happiness of society in general that women should have their understanding cultivated and enlarged as much as possible... Whatever women learn, let them be taught accurately... let a woman know one thing completely and she will have sufficient understanding to learn more."*

She shared Rousseau's view that the ideal education *"would consist in uniting health and agility of body with cheerfulness and activity of mind"*, and her practical contribution was to raise enormously the standard of writing for girls and women, in her stream of morally improving books for children, some of which were set in Bristol.

But neither Hannah More nor Edgeworth, bluestockings both, had a great deal of influence on the course of girls' education, which was not to improve for nearly a century. In 1854, the street directory shows there were 42 private day and boarding schools for girls; they were run mostly by spinsters who themselves had had similar schooling, and most of them only lasted for a few years before failing.

What they offered was a smattering of everything, which was in fact all that most parents required, because by this time no middle-class girl was going to have a career unless forced to by poverty. The vast majority were expected to marry and marry, if possible, above their social class. It was not to be until the 1860s that at last the right questions were asked by government: what were girls being educated for, and were they any less capable intellectually than their brothers?

What was so pernicious about the system was that girls - and to a lesser extent boys - were educated according to their social status, and not their intelligence or ability. If they were poor working class girls, they needed only basic literacy and the ability to cook, clean and sew, because regardless of intelligence, these girls could only hope to be servants.

This was the philosophy of Bristol's charity schools for girls, Red Maids, founded in 1634, Redcliff Blue Girls, (1720), and Elbridge's on St. Michael's Hill, (1738), right up to the reforms forced on the city by the 1864 Taunton Commission inquiry and subsequent legislation on endowed schools. (Bristol's endowed schools asked to be exempted from this investigation, but were refused).

Red Maids, one of the city's famous Hospital Schools, had opened in 1634 for *"40 poore women Children"* who would be *"taught to read English and to sowe or do some other laudable worke towards Theire*

The Red Maids' School in Denmark St, by an anonymous artist, c.1840

maintenance." Pupils were taken from the age of eight to 18, an extraordinarily long span if they were only to learn to become servants or apprentices.

The regime was harsh: until the 1840s they slept two to a bed for warmth, rose at six, did the housework, and the proceeds from their sewing work went to the headmistress. The girls were taught to read, but strangely not to write, and were allowed little fun or relaxation or exercise. (The status of the school was tellingly illustrated by the fact that in Regency times, Regent House, an expensive school at Bath, kept a Red Maids-style uniform which girls were made to wear as a punishment!).

Things improved when their old insanitary building in Denmark Street was replaced by a purpose-built one with warm water, heating and a bathroom, but the quality of the education was still poor. Even so, the school was not cheap: in the 1860s it emerged that Red Maids cost £3,000 a year to run - a lot to pay for teaching the girls as little as possible, to know their place, and to produce servants for Clifton, as the Western Daily Press sourly commented. The inspection by the Commissioner Joshua Fitch in 1864 did not produce a flattering picture of the endowed school:

> *" The educational aim in schools of this class is never high, The life lived in them is for the most part joyless and uninteresting. The children are dressed in a hideous costume, they are subject to many restraints of a humiliating kind which are presumed to be appropriate in a charity school.... the fact that all the scholars come from one class, and that a low one, causes the tone of thinking and of social life to become narrow and enervating and the absence of stimulus or supervision from without renders the teachers satisfied with educational results of the most meagre kind."*

Red Maids in uniform: from far left, 1869 and 1905

As a result of this damning report, the school was upgraded in 1871 to give a more general education. From then on, some of the pupils entered public examinations and were destined for training college, but it was not until 1911 that Red Maids appointed its first graduate teacher.

Marion Webb, who was headmistress from 1906 to 1934, finally succeeded in modernising the school, with the move to the current building at Westbury-on-Trym, by giving the girls a more up-to-date and comfortable uniform, a better diet, a proper library, and more freedom, with a less harsh regime and a wider, more rewarding curriculum, so that it some ways it became more like a high school.

But what really changed education for women in Bristol was, paradoxically, the arrival of Clifton College in 1862. Parents saw the effect of a good classical education on their sons, and began to think that it ought to be possible for daughters to be educated in the same way. After all Cheltenham had its Ladies College, for day girls as well as boarders, founded eight years earlier.

John Percival, the young and radical head of Clifton College, wanted such a school for his daughter Bessie, and there were other like-minded people living in Clifton who were interested in education for women. After a series of meetings, enough money was raised in subscriptions to start Clifton High School in 1877.

The high school movement which started in the late 1860s and early 1870s, was a new approach because the curriculum was much the same as for boys. Some headmistresses were against their girls entering competitive examinations, but they still wanted a rigorous course of study, and here at least the emphasis on mere accomplishments ended, and girls' minds were taken seriously.

Redland High School followed in 1882, and eventually as a result of the shake-up required by the Endowed Schools Act, a new endowed school for girls, Colston's, opened in 1891. Secondary state education for girls arrived at more or less the same time with the opening in the last decade of the century of Fairfield, St. George and Merrywood schools.

Parallel to this growth of education for girls was a movement to provide further education for women, again thanks to John Percival, who in 1868 founded the Association for the Promotion of Higher Education for Women. The arrival of Bristol University College in 1876, with its policy of admitting women to all courses (except as we shall see elsewhere, medicine) and the university's provision of extramural lectures for ladies, widened the horizons of many middle-class Bristol women and encouraged them to see that their daughters obtained proper schooling.
 That these new kinds of schools succeeded owed much to the first headmistresses who fought local prejudice and snobbery. Mary Alice Woods, first Head of Clifton High School, knew exactly what she was up against with the Clifton social mafia, who hated her ideas that classes should mix, and that the high school should be non-denominational. Teaching by lecture and blackboard was completely new to girls who had suffered the sterile learning by rote system at private schools, and doting mothers at first feared their daughters would get the dreaded "brain fever." In addition, the high school girl was popularly regarded by some as a mannerless hoyden who put herself morally at risk by using public transport. She played rough male games like cricket and hockey and grew up with opinions which made her far too independent and adventurous in mind and body.

Redland High School

The famous 18th C. façade of Redland High School

At Redland High School, founded in 1882, partly because Clifton was too far away for Redland girls to attend the new high school there, the first headmistress, Miss Elizabeth Ann Cocks also had radical notions. She actually took school parties to Paris in 1889, and insisted when she was appointed that the governors provided a library for the teachers, as well as a stock of chemicals for a yet to be built laboratory. Another milestone was the election of the first woman governor, Emily Sturge. By 1888, the first Redland High School girls had passed their Higher Examinations and were entering university.

But at first, teaching girls previously educated at home or in an academy was hard work. *"Many of the girls who come to us have been allowed to grow up to 13, 14 or even 15 years of age without ever having done any difficult or serious work"* was the complaint about some of the earliest entrants. The girls were not very fit either, so games were encouraged, for Miss Cocks believed that physical exercise aided girls *"in attaining a higher standard of energy and courage in mental work."*

Colston's

The imposing Victorian gateway of Colston's Girls School

The other new force in education for girls came with Colston's Girls' School, which was purpose-built, and which took in 205 girls aged six to 15 in the year it opened, 1891. The first headmistress, Georgina Smith, decided right from the start that her qualified teaching staff would specialise in subjects and teach them to all forms, so that all the girls could be taught to examination level. Though a master had to be appointed to teach chemistry, the governors hoped that eventually the staff would be all female.

Though the high school movement was unstoppable, approval of these changes was far from universal. ***The Girls' Own Paper***, in 1882, published a long article on the *Disadvantages of Higher Education For Women*:

> *It is a well-known fact that a woman's physique is not equal to a man's, and the brain power depends very much on the physique which nourishes the brain - ergo the average woman will never equal the average man on his own ground... while girls are learning Greek and mathematics they have little time for needle-work, which used to be part of every girl's education, and which they will want to understand at some time in their lives. It is the fashion now rather to sneer at darning, mending and other trifling household duties; but if a woman is to be a wife and mother she will need a great deal of such knowledge...It has yet to be proved that Cambridge examinations assist women in their household duties.*

ESTABLISHMENT FOR YOUNG LADIES,

CHESTERFIELD VILLA,

WESTBOURNE PLACE,

VICTORIA PARK, CLIFTON.

CONDUCTED BY MRS. CURTIS.

Formerly Pupil of Herz, De Coigney, and Professor Levi; and many years Governess in the Families of the Earl of Aylesford, and the Baron de Galz Malvirade, Paris—whose daughters' education she finished.

In introducing the above Establishment to the notice of the Christian Public, MRS. CURTIS begs to state that the principal objects of her unremitting attention, are—

First—To impart to her Pupils a sound *religious* education, founded on the obvious meaning of God's holy word.

Secondly—To convey a thorough knowledge of each department of a *useful* and an *accomplished* education, comprising English in all its branches, Music, Singing, French, Italian, German, Drawing, Painting, etc., etc. And—

Thirdly—By regular habits—frequent walks and recreative amusements, by a liberal table, and uniformly kind, affectionate treatment;—in a word, by combining as much as possible with the discipline of school the comforts and enjoyments of home, to promote the *health* and secure the *happiness* of her Pupils.

The situation is one of the most eligible in this delightful locality, and within a few minutes' walk of the Down.

The Young Ladies have the advantage of constantly speaking French with a resident Parisienne; and also of attending Lectures on Philosophical subjects, (illustrated by suitable and interesting experiments, with complete sets of first rate apparatus,) delivered by Mr. CURTIS, M.C.P., who also gives instruction in Writing, Arithmetic, the Classics, and the Mathematics.

TERMS PER ANNUM:

For Board, Music, French, and every department of English .. .. } *Thirty Guineas.*

Singing, Drawing, Italian, German, and other Accomplishments, at the Professors' charges ..

Laundress .. .. *Four Guineas.*

REFERENCES kindly permitted to the Parents of Pupils now under MRS. CURTIS's care.

An 1880's advertisement for the type of typical young ladies' educational establishment in Bristol which was not to survive for much longer

The Taunton Commission Report on secondary education for girls concluded: *"The general deficiency in girls' education is stated with the utmost confidence and with entire agreement. There was a want of thoroughness and foundation, want of a system; slovenliness and showy superficiality; inattention to the rudiments, and those not taught intelligently or in any scientific manner; want of organisation - these may sufficiently indicate the character of the complaints we have received... The girls' schools are inferior to the boys, though the essential capacity for learning is the same...".*

The private academies refused to be inspected. Yet these piffling private academies persisted for a long time - in the 1870s there were a staggering 107 of them in Bristol, most of them for girls and the majority of them in Clifton. "The healthiness and beauty of Clifton has rendered it a very favourite situation for ladies' schools, and the number of them is very large" wrote Catherine Winkworth in a section on Higher Education For Women in Bristol And its Environs, published in 1875. She noted that some schools did send pupils (boys) to sit the Oxford Local Examinations in Bath, and that since 1861 Bristol had had a centre for pupils wishing to take the equivalent Cambridge examinations which had been open to girls since 1865.

The End of an Era

The academic success of the high schools and the proof that girls could pass examinations and soon gain places at university, gradually killed the worst schools off, except for a handful which could offer a better quality education. A few of the Clifton academies did survive: Duncan House, founded in the 1880s in Clifton, lasted until the 1980s, and St. Joseph's, a Catholic high school for girls, later La Retraite, ran from 1905 until 1982.

There was also the Clergy Daughters School, another charitable boarding school, which was founded in Gloucester in 1831, and moved to Bristol in 1836. The school operated in Great George Street until the turn of the century, when it was renamed St. Brandon's; it subsequently moved to Clevedon and closed down in 1991.

Another survivor was Badminton, founded in 1858, making it one of the oldest boarding schools for girls in the country; until 1911 it was a typical seminary type school where girls had to wear corsets, and veils to protect their complexions. But with the arrival of a new headmistress, Beatrice Baker, in 1911, all that changed; socialism and internationalism became the rule and Badminton became a progressive, academic school for the daughters of upper middle class Fabians. There were debates and pottery classes and games on the Downs, and reading classes; in the Thirties Basque refugees from the Spanish Civil War came to the school, to be joined later by Czechs and German Jews fleeing the Nazis.

And in the 1990s, when co-education, even at the great public schools, is the norm, the pioneering Bristol high schools for girls are still flourishing, and achieving the outstanding academic results that their Victorian founders dreamed of a century ago.

Catherine Winkworth (1827 - 1878)

Catherine Winkworth is another key figure in the development of education for Bristol girls - indeed it was said that she wore herself to death in her efforts to get Clifton High School established. She and her social worker sister Susannah came to Bristol from Manchester in 1864, and immediately involved themselves in the various women's movements that were stirring at that time.

Catherine had been a delicate child, intellectually precocious, and especially close to her mother after the family moved to Manchester where the three youngest children were born. (Susanna and Emily remained in London to be 'educated' by their aunt Eliza.) The girls' mother died in 1845, and their father re-married not long afterwards, both of which events must have been quite a shock to the family. At this time the sisters got to know Mrs Gaskell, who thought that the girls' homelife was as unhappy as hers had been in similar circumstances, and who portrayed an insensitive stepmother in her novel, Wives and Daughters. Susanna was later, however, to portray their stepmother in a more favourable light.

Catherine's education was broadened by a stay in Dresden with aunt Eliza, where she studied music and German. Back in Manchester Catherine took further lessons run by Mr Gaskell, and studied logic with James Martineau, ex-pupil of Lant Carpenter in Bristol. The Unitarian connections were wide, and through James the sisters met Mary Carpenter before their move to Bristol, and James' feminist sister Harriet, whom they much admired. Susanna even became a Unitarian, like her new friends, and took an interest in social work. Through Mrs. Gaskell, Catherine also became a friend of Charlotte Brontë.

Catherine specialised in translation of German (her most famous work was the *Lyra Germanica*, a collection of translations of hymns, an achievement which is commemorated on a plaque in Bristol Cathedral), and it was natural that she should move in Clifton's intellectual and literary circle. Through this she met the young headmaster of the new Clifton College, John Percival, who in 1868 began to concern himself with the education of women.

They had at this stage just been allowed to join evening classes but only in selected and suitable subjects, but after 1868, middle class women were able to go to morning lectures in Clifton, on subjects as diverse as Astronomy, Political Economy, Logic, Physiology, and Music; there were also a series of classes on English Literature, Greek, Latin, Harmony, Botany, and Physical Geography.

"It was considered quite daring to attend these lectures" recalled Elizabeth Sturge. "We read diligently and every week handed in papers signed by a number or a pseudonym - such was the dread at that time of having your name known in such a connection. There was great excitement when the lists were read out - some who had not attained the position they had hoped for, were even known to weep!"

Catherine Winkworth became honorary secretary of the Association for Promoting the Higher Education of Women, organising lectures and obtaining visiting speakers, and by the early 1870's the classes were extended to take girls preparing for the Higher Cambridge Examination. The franker mature students admitted that they went in order to find interesting topics for conversations at Clifton dinner parties....

But initially, Miss Winkworth was conservative about the education of girls. "Miss Emily Davies (a pioneering educationist) has been here, about a College for Ladies and I was asked to one or two meetings about that, but got convinced that I didn't approve of it, except for teachers and exceptionally clever and studious girls..."

Nevertheless she threw herself into the establishment of Clifton High School - though she was anxious that the girls should not be "over-tired" - and eventually became a governor of Red Maids and a member of the Cheltenham Ladies College Council, a position Susannah Winkworth held after her sister's death in 1878 at the age of only 51. In her memory a scholarship was established for women attending Bristol University, a new Hall of residence has been named after her, and a plaque has recently been unveiled outside her house in Cornwallis Crescent, Bristol.

Emily Sturge (1842 - 1883)

No account of advances in education in Bristol at this time would be complete without further mention of the six Quaker Sturges sisters, whom we have already encountered in Chapter 1. They provided a model of female Victorian enlightened pioneering, forming part of a Bristol social group which Josephine Butler called a "corps d'elite, by which she meant especially those working for the repeal of the Contagious Diseases Act, Mary Estlin, The Priestman sisters and Margaret Tanner, although they would also have known the Winkworths, Mary Carpenter and Octavia Hill.

Emily achieved much in what was to be a tragically short life. She was born in 1842 and was the first of the girls to be sent to a boarding school in Weston-super-Mare which provided a happy and caring environment although, like most Dame Schools at that time, the education was limited. Education for its own sake and for others was always to interest her. She began by teaching at the Quaker Friends' Sunday School in Bristol. Then in 1868 the Clifton Association for Promoting the Higher Education of Women started university-type classes, and Emily and her other sisters eagerly took advantage. A variety of subjects, including maths and science, were offered and studied with enthusiasm; papers were written each week and handed in with trepidation. For intelligent young women who had had a limited education, these lectures must have been extremely challenging, and paved the way for subsequent lectures provided by the University College after it opened in 1876.

Clifton Hill girls in the first residential hall for women

From then on, education was to be Emily's major interest, although she was also active in the Liberal Association and Suffrage movement, becoming an experienced public speaker. This accomplishment stood her in good stead when she was invited to stand as a candidate for election to the Bristol School Board in 1880. Ratepayers, including women, could vote for what was a precursor of the local Education Authority. Her sister Elizabeth supported Emily at meetings and wrote: "She was a good speaker and made an excellent impression on the various audiences we found assembled in dingy club-rooms in the upper storeys of public houses, where many of these meetings were held."

Emily came second in the poll and joined the board, the youngest member by far at the age of 33. She devoted much time to the School Board, visiting schools regularly, supporting and advising staff and encouraging pupils by praise and prizes: a forerunner of today's School Governors. She remained on the Board to see a huge advance in the education of girls and training of teachers. She also became a warm supporter of the suffragette movement. As she said: *There is nothing in the accident of sex which in any way disqualifies us; if women do not exercise their responsibility they would remain as half developed creatures in a state of mental childhood.*

The newly opened University College was going through hard times and it was possible that the Chairs of English and History would have to be abolished. This would have been a disaster for women Arts students and threatened the evening classes for teachers from elementary schools working for their teachers' certificates. These evening classes had, in fact, been abolished, but Emily used her influence as a member of the school board to have then reinstated, with the proviso that there must be 35 entries. Numbers were achieved when the syllabus of the Teacher's Certificates were revised to put new emphasis on the teaching of English, History and Geography, at the expense of the more traditional 'women's subjects of French and German.

Emily then set about raising money for the threatened professorial posts at the University by organising an appeal to past and present students. The Student's Endowment Fund was set up, and within three years over £2000 had been collected, with additions from the proceeds of annual lectures. The strength of support helped to save the threatened Chairs.

In 1883 Emily became the first woman member of the Council of Redland High School, where she was described as "a tower of strength to the Council." She gave a scholarship for a girl to study science at the Merchant Venturer's College, and generally encouraged further education for the girls.

Shortly before her tragic death in 1883 she was involved in the setting up of a Day Training College in Bristol for teachers in elementary schools. She did not live to see its opening in 1892 under Marian Pease. She had been riding with her sister Helen when her horse bolted down Rownham Hill, on the Somerset side of the Suspension Bridge. Emily was thrown from her horse and died of a head injury later the same day.

Marian Pease 1859-1954

Marian Pease was not only one of the first students to enter the University College Bristol when it opened in 1876, but the University's Department of Education was formed on the basis of the Day Training College for Teachers in Berkeley Square, of which she was Mistress of Method. This title comprised the development of the curriculum, hostels for students and the care of their welfare, both physical and moral, lecturing and management of staff. Quite an undertaking for a young woman of 33!

In the spring of 1876, seventeen year old Marian was to have sat for the London University Women's examination, then the only London examination open to women. She must have been bitterly disappointed when prevented by an attack of scarlet fever. In compensation her parents decided that she should enter for one of the three scholarships for women offered by the new University College, Bristol.

Marian was the second child of Thomas Pease, a Quaker industrialist, and his third wife Susan, née Fry. It was Susan who was to create a happy family out of fifteen step-brothers and sisters, ten of which were her own. Marian had the advantage of sharing a tutor with her elder brother, Edward (later a co-founder of the Fabian Society) and with her step-brothers and sisters, and this fostered her life-long interest in mathematics. She had listened with interest to the older girls giving an account of the Extension Lectures in Bristol and reading the essays that they had written. In spite of these advantages her education had been patchy. She was the only scholarship candidate to offer mathematics, but in her reminiscences she comments on the kindness of Mr Rowley (later Professor) who gave her a viva in English Literature and when she disclaimed knowledge of a number of books he mentioned "he limited his questions to the very few I had read."

Marian was successful in winning the scholarship, as were Emily Pakeman and Amy Elizabeth Bell with her. The latter really should have had a chapter to herself. She was an Indian Mutiny orphan and after many adventures was brought by her Indian nurse, or Ayah, to the safety of her uncle's home. He was Colonel Goodeve, who lived at Cooks Folly, then the only house on the Downs overlooking the Avon Gorge. Eventually this delicate but intrepid woman became a stockbroker, and although defeated in her efforts to gain admission to the Exchange she operated successfully from a near-by office.

At Bristol Marian studied English Literature, Heat, Light and Sound and Advanced Mathematics in her first year. Classes in the latter subject were held at nine o'clock three mornings a week, and Marian has left us this description of her journey to College. *"I left home a few minutes after eight o'clock carrying my heavy bag of books - there were no lockers then - walked across Durdham Down, met Amy Bell who came in a cab from Stoke Bishop and then we took the horse tram from the bottom of Blackboy Hill to the top of Park Street. There were, of course no omnibuses or trams to Westbury in those days and the gas lamps only reached as far as the White Tree. The journey had its difficulties on dark, wet and windy winter mornings and afternoons."*

Hard work in poor surroundings was balanced by an enthusiasm which we in a more cynical age may envy. There was only a stuffy cloakroom in which the women students studied and ate their lunch, with the smell of rotten eggs percolating the building from the chemistry laboratory in the attics. Here, with new friends, Marian says she spent the happiest hours of her life.

Mr Marshall, a Fellow of St John's College Cambridge, was appointed Principal at Bristol in 1877. Marian gives a vivid description of his inaugural lecture on ecomomics. *"He spoke without notes and his face caught the light from the window while all else was in shadow. That lecture seemed to me the most wonderful I had ever heard. He told us of his faith that economic science had a great future in furthering the progress of social improvement, and his enthusiasm was infectious. I think the whole audience must have listened as breathlessly as I did."*

Marian attended Mr Marshall's regular classes on economics with her cousin, Mary Fry and a few other women, and found inspiration in his lectures and seminars. She and Mary were honoured to be given the task of reading some of the proof sheets of Marshall's 'Principles of Economics' and discussing with him points that were unclear. Equally stimulating was Mrs Marshall, who had been one of the first six students at the women-only Newnham College, and who had proved to anxious parents that higher education could be coupled with grace and charm. Her debating society was always lively and on one occasion when the subject was Irish Home Rule the clash between the supporters of Parnell and a group of young Irish women was such that the debate had to be adjourned. It was in this group that Marian first met Katharine Bradley and her niece Edith Cooper who settled in Clifton and wrote poetry under the name of 'Michael Field'. Marian graduated with honours in all subjects and was subsequently awarded an honorary Doctorate from the University in 1911.

Any question as to whether she should embark on a full-time career was settled by the economic necessity that faced her with the death of her father when she was twenty-four. She spent a year at the Cambridge Training College for teachers, and armed with its Certificate taught at the Birmingham City Day Training College for two years. By 1890, the Government's Department of Education had made provision for the recognition of Day Training Colleges for Teachers. Her Majesty's Inspector Dr J.G.Fitch encouraged Bristol

University College to set up a Committee to establish such a college which would admit young women for training, as well as making provision for the small group of girls in the University College working informally for the Cambridge Teacher's Certificate. At that time the alternative would be for girls to train at the Diocesan College at Fishponds, whose teaching and results had been castigated in a report by Mr Fitch: its Principals had graduated in theology from Oxford. Whatever their proficiency in theology, their knowledge of education was nil.

The great majority of teachers in Bristol Elementary Schools had qualified by attending the Bristol School Board Pupil-Teacher School, attending part-time. By the end of the century, the School was established in Broadmead with over 600 students. Those whose examination results showed them to be eligible were subsequently admitted to the Day Training College.

Professor Lloyd Morgan was by then Principal of University College Bristol and became Secretary of the Committee together with representatives of the Bristol School Boards and the Voluntary Schools. Emily Sturge was also one of its members. It was she who informed Marian that the Day Training College was to open and urged her to apply for the post of Mistress of Method. Sadly Emily Sturge was killed in a riding accident before the opening in October 1892.

From now on Marian devoted herself to the Training College, which was established at 21 Berkeley Square, with thirty students. Her uncle, Albert Fry, was Treasurer of the Council formed to run the College. He told Marian that she must not spend literally a shilling more than was absolutely necessary in furnishing and housekeeping, and "very meanly did we furnish" she later wrote.

By the age of 33, Marian was involved in the appointment of staff and day to day management as well as designing the curriculum, and preparing and delivering her own lectures. By 1909 she was recognised as a Special Lecturer in Education, a post that she held until 1928.

During the vacations she took groups of girls for reading parties in the Quantocks, usually near Alfoxden and Nether Stowey, where the Wordsworths and Coleridge had lived. Her own habits were spartan - like many Victorians she took a daily cold bath - but she was lavishly generous to others, and had an intense interest in people of all types. One of her students wrote, "she was to us a new kind of person. Everything seemed turned upside-down as there unfolded before our astonished eyes a new and larger world of mind and spirit than any we could have imagined."

Marian was becoming increasingly deaf and used an ear trumpet, but this did not limit her activities. The Training College was growing and new houses had to be acquired for student accommodation. A substantial dinner was provided in Berkeley Square where staff mixed with students and a letter in 1912 describes this as good for their health and manners. It is in this letter that Marian rejects the idea of a Refectory where women and men might mix. If there were to be one then she hoped that separate dining-rooms would be provided to avoid possible difficulties.

In addition to the Training College Marian opened a School for Mothers (the second in the city) and the first ante-natal clinic, both under Dr Lily Baker, an early gynaecologist, and supported the opening of the first Open-Air School. In 1880 she and her sisters, Rosa and Dora, opened a club for girls working in a factory in Barton Hill, with an entertainments programme of reading, writing and talking alternating with singing and dancing, and a short Quaker meeting to end the evening. By 1911 they were joined by others in purchasing three houses and thus laying the foundation for the establishment of the University Settlement, run by the University of Bristol..

It was in this area that the Worker's Educational Association (W.E.A) first became active. It was a social and charitable association to benefit the poor of Bristol, in particular of the Barton Hill area. Free lectures on all subjects were given, and Marian lectured on English Literature. As if all this were not enough, Marian was also a Governor of Sidcot (Quaker) School, the Red Maid's School from 1914 - 1939, a member of the League of Nations and, after 1945, of the U.N. Association!

After retirement in 1912 Marian moved to Almondsbury with her sister Rosa and there supervised a country cottage maintained by Badminton School to provide holidays for under-nourished or delicate children. In old age she lived with Rosa in Street, Somerset, eventually dying at the age of 95. She must have been gratified to see the Department of Education taking over the function of the Training College in Berkeley Square. In 1920 the University once more showed its farsightedness in appointing Helen Wodehouse to the new Chair of Education, one of the first women to hold such a post in a British University. It was a triumph for the young student of the University College to have achieved so much, and to be able to write *"I had the satisfaction and honour of becoming a member of the University before I retired and the great pleasure of attending the opening of the University by the King in 1925."*

3   The Healers: "An Outrage on all Modesty" (from a letter to The Lancet, November 1889)

1880 advert for The new Women and Children's hospital

For many centuries women played a primary role in treating illness. Wise women were the herbalists of their day as were the ladies in the manor houses with their herb gardens and still-rooms. In addition it was noted in the four-teenth century that women were in the Guild of Surgeons, and Edward III appointed a woman physician to look after his wife, Philippa of Hainault.

Perhaps their influence was becoming too great. In 1421 a Parliamentary edict was passed which included the clause that 'no women use the practice of Fisyk' on pain of long imprisonment'. This was a response to a petition from male physicians. At the same time the men were required to have graduated from University. The battle lines were drawn and discrimination ensued. Women were excluded from the diploma of the Royal College of Physicians who gained their Charter in 1518, and, later, were excluded from the Royal College of Surgeons.

A loophole was provided in 1815 by the Society of Apothecaries who laid down conditions for qualification: 5 years apprenticeship, a course of lectures and six months attendance at a hospital or dispensary; (in 1850 amended to 3 years of lectures and hospital attendance). It was stated that the Society would examine and licence any persons who fulfilled their requirements.

Bristol women were noted as early pioneers in medicine, the most famous of them being Elizabeth Blackwell (1821 - 1910), as the first woman doctor. The way was tested by Elizabeth Garrett, who reached the goal of sitting the final examination of the R.S.A. by a combination of nursing and private tuition. Initially the Society refused to examine her but gave way when her father threatened legal action on the grounds that the Charter referred to 'any person'. Elizabeth took the examination, became a Licentiate in 1865 and was placed on the Medical Register a year later. Quickly the loophole was closed. A resolution now required all candidates to have studied in a recognised medical school. Women were not excluded by the Society if they had attended medical school, but no medical school in Britain would accept women.

This was the situation when Eliza Walker Dunbar decided to study medicine and found all avenues in Britain closed to her. An account of her career is given in this section as is that of the last of our pioneering doctors, Beryl Corner, who successfully fought prejudice and discrimination 50 years later.

The creation of the University and Bristol Medical School

As we have seen, Bristol women had shown themselves ready and anxious to ally themselves with the Rev. John Percival, Headmaster of Clifton College, in the Association for the Higher Education of Women formed in 1868. A year later he founded the Association for the Promotion of Evening Classes before turning his attention towards the creation of a University for Bristol. In this he was supported by Benjamin Jowett, Master of Balliol, who offered support on two conditions: one was that Literature should be coupled with Science, and the second that women should be admitted on an equal basis with men.

A meeting was held in 1874 at the Victoria Rooms to discuss the project. Eminent men attended and influential local families gave their support. Most of these, however, were Non-conformists and Quakers such as the Frys, noted for Liberal views, rather than the Anglican Tories.

Repeatedly antagonism between these groups has hindered development in Bristol. Nevertheless, with minimal support from the Tories, the University College of Bristol opened in October 1876 in two houses in Park Row.

The Bristol Medical School had already been formally established in 1833. For nearly half a century, it too had been hindered by religious and political rivalries as well as by lack of money. However in 1879 it was affiliated to the University College and by 1893 a united Faculty formally joined the College. Women now turned their eyes to the study of medicine in Bristol, perhaps inspired by that indomitable Bristolian, Elizabeth Blackwell.

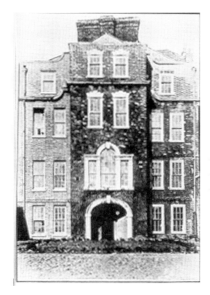

Lunsford House, reputed to be the first home of the Bristol Medical School

Elizabeth Blackwell (1821 - 1910)

Elizabeth Blackwell is possibly Bristol's most famous woman pioneer. She was born in 1821 in Counterslip, Bristol, to Hannah and Samuel Blackwell, a non-conformist couple who believed in equal educational possibilities for girls. The family moved to 1 Wilson St, off Portland Square, where in 1924 a plaque commemorating her was unveiled by Beryl Corner (the last of the women doctors portrayed in this chapter), together with a final year medical student.

In 1832 the family emigrated to America, only to be left poverty-stricken after Samuel's early death. Elizabeth and two of her sisters opened a boarding-school to help support their widowed mother and younger brothers. As the boys became independent, Elizabeth, who hated teaching, started studying with the aim of enrolling in a medical school. A friend had convinced her of the desperate need for women doctors to attend women: many suffered agonies and delayed treatment if their only recourse was to a man doctor.

In spite of, or perhaps because of, unanimous opposition, Elizabeth started studying and saving in order to enter a medical school. For two years she taught in schools by day, and gave music lessons in the evenings. In addition she taught herself Greek and studied anatomy and physiology, in what what she described as her 'spare time'.

Elizabeth applied to and was rejected by sixteen medical colleges before being admitted to Geneva College, New York State, where she graduated with distinction in 1849. Elizabeth next travelled to Paris where she enrolled in La Maternité as a student midwife to gain experience as an obstetrician. The fates were against her, however, when as she was syringing the eye of a baby that had become infected in the birth canal, pus from the baby's eye squirted into her own, and despite treatment the eye became blind. This avenue of medicine was then closed to her, because it involved close surgery.

Elizabeth Blackwell

Elizabeth returned to England and spent a period studying at St Bartholomew's in London. It is ironic to learn that she was generally welcomed, except by the Professor for the Diseases of Women. Did he fear the possibility of competition into what was then a closed shop? On returning to New York she met hostility and suspicion from both sexes, and suffered acutely from loneliness. In 1856 Elizabeth adopted a seven-year-old orphan, Kitty, educated her and gained a devoted companion for life. In her autobiography Elizabeth recalled Kitty's remark when a male doctor visited. "How very odd it is to hear a man called doctor!"

A group of Quaker women helped her set up a clinic in a slum area, and gradually her persistence and skill was rewarded. By 1857 she had established the New York Infirmary for Women and Children, which obtained a Charter as a medical school eleven years later. It was staffed entirely by women, with Elizabeth as director, her sister Emily (who had followed in her footsteps and qualified in 1856) as surgeon, and Dr Maria Zakrzewska (another pioneer), as physician. Shortly after the medical school had obtained its charter, a nursing school was opened. Elizabeth endowed a chair of Hygiene (or Preventative Medicine), and became its first professor. With this solid achievement behind her Elizabeth returned to England as Professor of Gynaecology at the London School of Medicine for Women, and became the first woman to be placed on the British Medical Register in 1859.

In 1869 she stayed in Bristol with Mary Carpenter's married sister at 2 George St. while attending the Social Science Congress with Mary Carpenter. They shared many friends; Florence Nightingale, Lady Byron and Frances Power Cobbe. Elizabeth must have appreciated the article written by Frances attacking male doctors for their lack of help to women, either those in the working classes or those in the fashionable world. "Did they ever make any serious effort to stop the senseless and health-destroying fashion of women's dress, the reckless dissipation and late hours which have sent thousands of thoughtless girls to their graves?"

The article continued to argue that the case is reversed, however, when one of the aims of the movement for the Higher Education of Women, would be to fit lady doctors to enter the market with the men who had hitherto monopolised the profits of the profession. Then, indeed, the doctors grew earnest and made a grand discovery - namely that "mental labour is peculiarly injurious to the weaker sex - much worse, it would appear, for their feeble constitutions, than any amount of ball-going and dissipion: and that in short, a term at Girton was worse than five London seasons. Women would perish and the human race cease to multiply if female intellects ascended from gossip to Greek."

In 1870 Elizabeth set up a private practice in London, and supported Elizabeth Garrett in the Dispensary that she had opened there. She had finally given up practising medicine herself due to her failing health, and retired to Hastings, but she did not stop campaigning for the welfare of children and prevention of disease.

In 1902 she and Kitty paid a final visit to Bristol, and four years later she visited America for the last time, to celebrate her sister Emily's eightieth birthday. She was joined by two nieces to make up a quartet of Blackwell doctors! Elizabeth died at home in Hastings in 1910, aged 89 - a pioneer of whom Bristol is rightly proud.

Emily Blackwell (1826 - 1910)

Elizabeth's younger sister Emily was also born in Bristol and educated in America, where she, too, qualified in medicine. She worked with Sir James Simpson, a gynaecologist and obstetrician, and pioneer of anaesthetics in childbirth , especially chloroform, which gained public acceptance when it was used by Queen Victoria.

Emily helped to open her sister's Dispensary in New York city, which she ran from 1869 to 1910, aged 84. From 1869 to 1899 she was Dean and Professor of Obstetrics and Diseases of Women at the Women's Medical College attached to the New York Infirmary founded by Elizabeth. She was the first woman doctor to undertake major surgery on a considerable scale.

The First Bristol Medical Students

It was not until 1891 that the first woman medical student was admitted to the physiology department of the University College by Professor Lloyd Morgan. She was then Miss Parry, later Lady Barrett, and regrettably was not allowed to study anatomy in Bristol. She moved to London where she qualified. The first woman to obtain a Bristol degree from the Medical School was Miss Katherine Cole, a Redland High School girl who had a London Honours Degree in Botany with Physiology as a subsidiary subject. When she applied to the Medical Faculty in Bristol in 1907 she was told that women were not admitted. With great satisfaction she was able to point out that she had taken the London degree from Bristol and thus had already been admitted to the Faculty for lectures and practical work in physiology. Among others, Rendle Short (later Professor of Surgery) supported her and opposition was eventually overcome. From then on women students were admitted.

Miss Cole had the support of her future husband, Reeve Heber, and in 1909 was joined in the Medical School by Miss Hilda Ewins. It was the same year in which the latter's future husband, Wilfred (Bill) Adams entered the school. The difficulties were great for these young women, especially as the rivalries between the two hospitals persisted. Whereas Miss Cole was fully accepted at the Bristol General Hospital Miss Ewins found considerable opposition in spite of being dresser to the friendly Rendle Short. A major problem was that she was not admitted to the Residents' dining-room with the men students, and was expected to have meals with the nurses at set times where punctuality was all-important; totally unsuitable for a medical student working erratic hours. At the end of three months, considerably slimmer, Miss Ewins transferred to the B.G.H. and enjoyed cold meat, pickles and rice pudding with the men in the students' dining-room. She spent a happy six months working in the General Hospital.

Back at the B.R.I. for in-patient surgery, difficulties recurred. Most of the surgeons refused to have her as a dresser but the idiosyncratic Irish surgeon, Mr Hugh Slack, accepted her, saying "I like freaks of all sorts". In spite of his support, problems arose over the need for students to 'sleep in'. This was unthinkable, so that complicated shifts were arranged, inconvenient for Miss Ewins and unpopular with the men students. A similar problem arose when she became a midwifery student, but by now the first World War had started and the need for women doctors was foreseen. A corner was eventually found in the Sister's room of an empty ward, with the Matron's comment, "It's quite unsuitable, as you will agree." Miss Ewin "was prepared by this time to sleep on a shelf, so was prompt to accept a whole room, however small and draughty", and she completed her training in spite of everything. (In 1946 the present author, L.B. had to fight to sleep in the Residents' quarters and share with the men doctors rather than be in the inconvenient Nurses' Home as proposed by the Matron.)

Following Miss Cole and Miss Ewins, a Miss Salter enrolled in 1912 and then Miss Elizabeth Casson. Both graduated in 1919. The number of women students steadily increased until by 1917 thirteen were admitted to Medical School, one of whom was Victoria Tryon. Elizabeth Casson, Victoria Tryon and Beryl Corner followed in the footsteps of the earliest pioneers and became experts in their particular field - all were awarded an honorary degree by Bristol University.

Eliza Walker Dunbar (1845 - 1925)

Until very recently the name "Walker Dunbar Hospital" could be seen on a house a few yards down from the Elizabeth Blackwell Nursing Home in Clifton Down Road, and for many years her portrait (now lost) hung in the hall. Elizabeth Blackwell, the first British woman doctor to qualify in medicine, is commemorated in Bristol, but surprisingly little is known about Eliza Walker whose pioneering life work was in Bristol.
Eliza Walker was born in 1845 in Bombay, the daughter of a surgeon in the Military Department and sister of Dr Dunbar Walker: (Dunbar was a family name adopted by Eliza in 1878). By the age of eleven she and her sister had left the heat of India to become pupils at the two-year-old Cheltenham Ladies' College.

Here Eliza came under the influence of one of the great pioneers in education, Miss Dorothea Beale, and, among other subjects, received a good grounding in German, leading to fluency in that language after she had completed her education in Frankfurt.

Her family background, her school and the example of contemporary pioneering women such as Elizabeth Backwell and Elizabeth Garrett must have all contributed to Eliza's decision to study medicine. Elizabeth Garrett was the first woman to study in Britain and to be placed on the Medical Register as a Licentiate of the Society of Apothecaries. Following her example, other women sought to enter medicine by this route.

In 1867 Louisa Atkins, Frances Morgan and Eliza Walker passed the preliminary examinations in Latin, geometry and history at Apothecaries' Hall and went on to study under Elizabeth Garrett at her dispensary. However this threat to the male monopoly in medicine at the time was soon countered. The Society of Apothecaries resolved that in future all candidates for their final examinations must have studied in a recognised medical school: at that stage all medical schools in England were for men only.

Eliza Walker Dunbar

Eliza, together with Louisa Atkins and Frances Morgan, decided to enter the medical degree course at the University of Zurich, which had been open to women since 1864. In 1872 she graduated and gained a M.D. for a thesis (in German) on embolism in arteries of the brain. She then took a post-graduate clinical course in Vienna for a year before she settled in Bristol, henceforth to be her adopted home. She was soon one of a circle of women who campaigned for Women's Suffrage: her friendship with Mary Carpenter must have dated from this time.

In 1873 she applied for a post as Resident Medical Officer at the Hospital for Women and Children, established on St Michael's Hill in 1861. The Appointment's Committee felt that "there would be a peculiar fitness in electing a lady to the vacant office", but wishing to avoid controversy they referred the matter to the Subscribers. On 11th June 1873 the meeting was held and the principle that appointments should be open to women was established. Thereupon the Committee appointed Eliza

Walker to the post. But they had not reckoned with the hostility of the medical establishment. Two of the Consultant Surgeons resigned forthwith.

Eliza didn't have long to enjoy her appointment. The records which would have given us details of the disagreement that quickly arose between her and one of the physicians, Dr. Ward Bush, have long since been lost by the hospital authorities. But it seems that Eliza had been reprimanded by Dr. Bush for a failure to carry out his orders, and that she had defended herself with " the use of many hasty expressions... in the heat of passion." We can only imagine what she told him. Male solidarity followed with all the physicians and surgeons refusing to work with Eliza - with the honourable exception of one Mr James. On 17th September Eliza wrote to the committee tendering her resignation, and the letter was published in the local and national press. Two letters of apology were also quoted, giving a picture of events:

(First apology to Dr Bush)

Hospital for Children, July 22nd
Sir. I beg to apologise for what seemed to you neglect of your patients. It was with no wish to show you any disrespect that I omitted, yesterday and to-day, to cauterise the little girl's throat, but because I did not know to what length of time your orders extended; and as you did not come to the Hospital, the case not being sufficiently urgent, I exercised a discretionary power, to which I believed, as house surgeon, I was entitled. Another time I shall inform myself more carefully of your wishes. I wish also to apologise for the many hasty expressions used by me to-day in the heat of passion. I am yours truly,
ELIZA WALKER

(Second apology to Dr Bush)

Hospital for Children. August 10th
Dr Walker, having heard that her first apology to Dr Bush was considered insufficient, begs to offer a more ample one. Dr Walker admits that it was an error of judgement to omit any part of the treatment of a case - thus the application of iodine and cauterisa-tion - without writing for permission to the acting honorary officer, but deprecates, by reasons already given, that there was any wilful insubordination on her part. Dr Walker applied iodine, as Dr Bush directed; but found on her visit next morning, that the nurse had made the application for that day. Knowing that the latter had been hurt at the unusual want of confidence, Dr Walker refrained from reproof. She was wrong in that, but especially in letting it

appear as if the nurse had acted under orders. Dr Walker regrets extremely that she so forgot her position as to make any answer to Dr Bush's threat and reproaches, she ought to have been entirely silent. She retracts all the injurious and disrespectful expressions that she made use of, and begs Dr Bush to consider that they were said under the influence of anger, and would not have been said in a calm temper. Dr Walker hopes that this apology may be thought sufficiently detailed.

A final quotation indicates the bitterness that she felt:

Some members of the staff, and Dr. Bush especially, professed to have recognised the principle that the office of house surgeon might be held by a woman. They must have known how important it was to the cause that I represent that the experiment of my appointment should prove successful. It behoved them, as gentlemen, to be lenient to a fault which few men have not at one time or another been guilty of, in consideration that in compelling my resignation they would injure not so much an individual, as a just cause which has as yet too few supporters. Moreover, although an outbreak of anger placed me at the mercy of Dr. Bush - of this as a natural consequence of my weakness I do not complain - it did not place me in the same relation to the rest of the staff. I am of the same profession as themselves; common courtesy, common fairness, commanded that I should be heard in my defence. The worst criminal is not judged unheard, and I think I could have shown that not all the provocation was on my side. I decline altogether to submit to their code of honour; their position I unhesitatingly challenge. Much as I may be to blame, I cannot charge myself with injustice, unfairness, and, as to neglect of duty, you know that without any notice they left the entire medical charge of the hospital and dispensary to chance and me.

Meanwhile **The Lancet** compared the situation in Bristol with that of Birmingham where Louisa Atkins had been appointed and where the medical officers were said to have been favourable. In Bristol the governors were said to have "forced a female subordinate" upon existing staff. The leader writer continues *"We cannot affect surprise at the result which has been attained, and do not see how any other could have been expected."*

The Lancet continues the battle against women doctors in a long article:

Women are neither physically nor morally qualified for many of the onerous, important, and confidential duties of the general practitioner; nor capable of the prolonged exertions or severe exposures to all kinds of weather which a professional life entail...

The real reasons for this passionate opposition to women in medicine become clear when it is urged that until women possess in a high degree all the qualifications necessary - (those qualifications denied them) - then "it is surely opposed to all principles of political and social economy to urge females into the field to the necessary exclusion of many men, for already the profession is overstocked."

There is no record of how Eliza spent the next few years other than a change of housing from Cotham Terrace to Sunderland Place where she lived and perhaps practised until her final move to 9 Oakfield Road in 1880.

The Read Dispensary

THE READ DISPENSARY, ST. GEORGE'S ROAD; 1907.

In spite of the initial setback, Eliza, supported by her friends, pressed on. The Dispensary movement supplemented the work of the Voluntary Hospitals in Bristol and in 1874 Miss Read founded the Read Dispensary for Women and Children in St George's Road, Hotwells, with Eliza Walker as the first Honorary Medical Attendant. At first the Dispensary opened twice a week, later daily, and women were charged an initial fee of one shilling and sixpence thereafter. The fee for children was sixpence and threepence respectively. Towards the end of the century these charges were not inconsiderable, especially for a woman with many children, but the need for access to medical care was vital. Slum housing and malnutrition allowed infectious diseases to take their toll, and epidemics of typhoid fever, scarlet fever, diptheria and cholera swept through the city. When public health measures had reduced these epidemics it was only to reveal the high loss of maternal life during pregnancy and childbirth, and of babies under one year of age.

We can imagine Eliza on fine days walking from her home in Oakfield Road and passing through Berkeley Square on her way to the slums of Hotwells. She had recognised the need for a hospital for women and children to be staffed by women, and where better could it be sited than in this part of Clifton where prevailing south-westerly winds blew across the fields of Brandon Hill, clearing away the smoke and mist rising from the insalubrious dock area below? Once more the ladies of the Committee of the Read Dispensary gathered together, approved the scheme and gathered the necessary funds for the purchase of a house. New buildings had been erected on the open southern side of Berkeley Square and one of these was found to be suitable.

In December 1895 the Hon. Lewis Fry opened the Bristol Private Hospital for Women and Children at 34 Berkeley Square with an associated house in Charlotte Street. Next day two patients were admitted and within a month it became clear that more beds were required and eight were added to the original six. By June 1896 there had been twenty-eight patients, two of whom came from some distance, having suffered for ten and fourteen years respectively while awaiting surgery by a woman doctor. Three years previously *The Lancet* had asserted that "the idea of female attendants is positively repulsive to the more thoughtful women of this country!"

Eventually even more accommodation was needed and to obtain this the Hospital was transferred to a large house in Clifton Down Road where thirty beds and two cots were provided. This was opened in June 1931 by Lady Barrett, M.D.,C.B.E.and was then known as the Walker Dunbar Hospital.

Associated with Eliza were two other women doctors who attended both the Read Dispensary and the Hospital. Emily Eberle, a member of a well-known Bristol family, who had been appointed a Honorary Surgeon to the Out-patients of the Bristol Children's Hospital between 1897-1905 lived at 17 Oakfield Road, while Dr. Marion Linton lived at number 21. The Hospital Treasurer, Miss Talbot, was at Merton Lodge in the same road. Sharing the house with Eliza was Miss St John who taught at Redland High School. It is tempting to picture this group of friends and colleagues meeting in the evening after work, when, it is hoped, they allowed themselves some relaxation. For as well as her work at the Dispensary, the Hospital and her practice in her home Eliza was also the visiting medical officer to the Red Lodge Reformatory School and to the Bristol Training College for teachers in Berkeley Square. Eliza was not only a sponsor for the Bristol Suffrage Movement but was allied with Emily Sturge and the Priestman sisters in the formation of the Bristol Association of Working Women, which provided a link between suffragists and the labour movement. She was medical adviser to the Association.

In addition to her immediate colleagues in Oakfield Road were her neighbours, Mr Cyril Walker, an opthalmic surgeon and his wife Dr Caroline Walker. The latter had qualified in medicine after considerable difficulties, gaining her M.D in Brussels in 1896. She was active in

The Walker Dunbar Hospital

Bristol both in medicine and social work fields and was especially valued for her wise and balanced advice during the fifteen years that she was chairman of the Walker Dunbar Hospital Committee.

Eliza continued to practise until her death following a fall in her 80th year in 1925. Her gross estate was only three and a half thousand pounds, and one can only conjecture that most of what she earned was spent on the causes for which she had worked. The obituary in the Medical News of 1925 is a fitting contrast to the articles in The Lancet in 1873:

> *This wonderful and kindly old lady will be much missed by all who had the good fortune to know her or be under her care ...to the end of her career she showed as outstanding qualities courage, perseverance and pluck. She gathered round her, and retained throughout her life, a devoted band of friends and supporters.*

Vicky Tryon (1897 - 1977)

Older inhabitants of Bristol still remember Vicky Tryon as a dedicated GP. For more than 40 years she did her rounds on her bicycle, or could be seen trudging through the snow, a heavy bag in each hand. She was not domesticated but relied on a housekeeper and thus was available to her patients at any time of day or night, sleeping on a couch in the hall while awaiting a midwifery call. A patient recalls "I ran across Clifton Down with my coat over my nightdress as my flatmate was desperately ill with an asthma attack. Vicky did not hesitate. She grabbed her bag and ran back with me at all speed, and on up five flights of stairs. She saved my friend's life."

Vicky Tryon

Vicky always maintained that she needed very little sleep and would do late visits as long as there was a light on in the house. Indeed a contemporary says "if she visited you before 10pm you knew that you were really ill".

She was born in Bristol, the youngest of six children, and educated at Clifton High School. She was a lively undergraduate at Bristol University, and became Woman President of the Union in 1919. (There were separate men and women presidents until 1971). A year later she was senior student at Clifton Hill House. These posts did not transform Vicky into a dignified young lady. There had been a history of rowdyism at Degree ceremonies prior to the War, and Vicky encouraged its resumption. Singing and shouting interrupted the proceedings and on one occasion a hen was let loose to fly over the heads of the assembled students and dignitaries.

An account is given of Vicky in her final year journeying in a fellow-student's car to Ham Green Hospital. Beyond the Suspension Bridge the road was blocked by male students cycling along at a snail's pace - cars were rare then and a woman student with a car even rarer. Vicky became exasperated by the hold-up, leapt out of the car, picked up one of the obstructing cyclists, deposited him in a ditch and jumped back into the car to complete the journey.

Victoria Tryon graduated in 1922 and, with three other women, applied for the post of House-surgeon at the General Hospital. It was with great reluctance that the Hospital Committee agreed to interview the women and then only on condition that they would agree to call one of the men residents if in difficulty... It was with equal reluctance that the women candidates agreed to this after 24 hours of soul-searching. Victoria was appointed 'on probation', and did so well without the help of the men that the consultant surgeon deliberately chose women for subsequent appointments.

Following this probationary period Vicky put up her plate at 3 Harley Place, Clifton and gained the affection of her many patients. She delivered many hundreds of babies in Clifton, at first often without the assistance of a midwife. She not only looked after the mothers but gave much confidence to anxious fathers. She always cared for her patients with great competence, unremitting care and compassion, especially for the old and lonely, with whom she would sometimes sit up far into the night.

For many years she was Medical Officer to Badminton School, where the girls punned affectionately on her name and called her 'the Tripod'. She was also medical officer to Clifton Hill House, only giving up the latter when a woman doctor was appointed to the Student Health Service. She was also an Honorary Physician to the Read Dispensary and the Walker Dunbar Hospital.

The Soroptomists

From 1927 - 28 Vicky was president of the Soroptomists Club of Bristol. This had been started as a professional women's offshoot of the Rotary Club, in 1920. Initially called the Venture Club, it was an extremely popular institution and reached 114 members in its first year, meeting regularly at Clifton High School. The first president was the inspiring Miss Eleanor Addison, headmistress of Clifton High school. Meanwhile, against a background of increasing alarm in America over the new liberties in manners and dress that women were taking, the Venture Club idea had crossed the Atlantic. A club for professional women was formed in Oaklands, California, called the Soroptomists club. The first president was Violet Chardsen Ward, a great fighter for equal pay for women. she determined what the path of the movement would be: a service organisation with strong international links, aiming to promote international understanding and goodwill.

By 1922 clubs had been founded across America, the movement's first victorious campaign being the protection of the giant Redwood trees. By 1927 the movement had spread to Paris, where the founder member was Suzanne Noel, a pioneer plastic surgeon, and from there to Holland, Italy, Austria, Germany, China and Japan. In 1930 the ten original ladies' Venture clubs in Britain amalgamated with the movement, which is now represented in 119 countries, with over 3,000 clubs. The Bristol club under Vicky specialised in help for the unemployed during the Recession, homeless women in Bedminster, and children without mothers.

In 1951 Vicky was elected first woman President of the Bristol Medico-Chirurgical Society, and in 1977 she was given the Honorary Degree of Master of Arts in recognition of her work, a remarkable honour for a general practitioner. Like many of our pioneer women she was unmarried and died at the ripe old age of 87, having devoted her life completely to her work.

Elizabeth Casson (1881 - 1954)

Elizabeth Casson in early and later life.

Elizabeth Casson, or Elsie as she was known in her family, was another of Bristol's pioneering doctors. At a time when there was little provision for the treatment of mental illness, she bought and established Dorset House, on the Promenade, for private patients of limited means. Her methods were what we would now call holistic (including homeopathy) and out of them arose the nationally and internationally acclaimed school of Occupational Therapy, still called Dorset House, but now situated in Oxford. In 1926 she became the first woman to gain a Doctorate at Bristol, and in 1951 she was awarded an OBE.

'Elsie' was born in Denbigh in 1881 the sixth of seven children, one of whom was Lewis Casson, the well-known actor. Elsie, as Elizabeth was always known to her family, had an idyllic childhood in the unspoilt country near Denbigh, surrounded by many aunts, uncles and cousins. Her parents were affectionate and devout, but not rigorously so.

Although brought up in largely non-conformist Wales, the sectarian nature of many of the chapels was not to the taste of the Cassons, and Elsie remained an Anglican.

Her father Thomas Casson was initially a bank manager in Denbigh, a boring occupation from which he escaped by building an organ factory in London, which was, unfortunately for his family, a less lucrative occupation. Elsie attended a mediocre school, and soon after the move the youngest member of the family, Annie, died of scarlet fever. Elsie was miserable. North London was a poor exchange for North Wales, and in addition there was insufficient money for her to train as a teacher; reluctantly she took a secretarial course at Pitman's.

For a time Elsie worked as a secretary to her father. After he retired she became a secretary to Octavia Hill, and learned about the management of slum property. Her niece, Nancy, described her work:

> *Elsie was interested in the houses. Access could be improved by a staircase here, a door-way knocked there, a bridge across. A dark place could have a window. She also accepted the tenants. The property might be full of bed-bugs and fleas. The tenants' heads might be full of lice, the drains blocked. All would be corrected, provided the rent was paid. Mill Hill might pay a child to scrub for a neighbour so that the mother could pay the rent, but if it was not paid, out went the tenant.*

At this time she was also secretary to the Red Cross in Southwark. This, together with her work for Octavia Hill, may have led her to the decision, at the age of thirty, to study medicine. Her uncle, Sir Isambard Owen, was then Vice-Chancellor of Bristol University, and told her that she would be admitted if she matriculated. While continuing with her charitable work, she settled down to study, passing all her subjects easily - with the exception of Latin. The extended family came to her aid with extra coaching, until she eventually passed after two years' struggle. In 1914 she became a student at Bristol, living in Clifton Hill House, and she graduated in 1919.

Elsie spent a year in the West Herts hospital as Resident Medical officer, before deciding to specialise in psychiatry, and became a medical officer at the Royal Holloway Sanitorium in 1921. The Holloway Sanitorium was an impressive Gothic institution set in 24 acres of grounds. It is now a Grade 1 listed building. It was run on kindly but Victorian lines, hierarchical, and with a strict etiquette. Here Elsie had her quarters, in which she enjoyed entertaining members of her family. Here she gained a wide experience of mental illness, and passed the Diploma in Psychological Medicine in 1922. Four years later she eventually gained her Doctorate at Bristol University, the first woman to do so. The following year, in 1927, she won the Gaskell Prize and Gold medal in psychological medicine.

In 1930 Elsie returned to Bristol. At that time, mentally ill patients were either housed in the large asylum or, if wealthy enough, in one of the private nursing homes. Elsie realised that there was a need for a private clinic for those of more limited means. She found Dorset House, a four storey building a stone's throw from the Clifton Suspension Bridge. This bridge, noted for its attraction to the suicidal, must have been a challenge, but Elsie was determined that her patients should feel free. Bravely she chose this building where doors and windows would remain open, and where trust and vigilance would replace the bunches of keys and locked doors that were typical of asylums of the time.

However, to buy Dorset House, she needed money. Her brother, Lewis Casson, was on a theatrical tour of South Africa with his famous wife, Sybil Thorndyke, when he received a cable from Elsie which read "Can you lend me a thousand pounds?" The reply was economical and to the point: "Yes".

Although her work at Dorset House was particularly noted for the development of Occupational Therapy, there were other aspects of the life there. Elsie was far ahead of her time when she created a community comprised of staff and patients, regardless of rank or status. She built up a dedicated group of workers who also joined in all the informal activities, such as dancing, drama and country outings. For she wrote that "Occupational Therapy can use any occupation that aids recovery - games, music, dancing, reading and acting plays, picnics, and other expeditions..."

Dorset House

Elsie's interest in Occupational Therapy was first aroused when, arriving at the women's wards in hospital after a weekend, she noticed that "The atmosphere had completely changed ... preparations for Christmas had begun ... and patients were using all their talents with real interest and pleasure. I knew from that moment that such occupation was an integral part of treatment and must be provided."

At that time Occupational Therapy barely existed in Britain, but Elsie was very impressed when visiting the Bloomingdale Hospital in America. "The whole atmosphere of a mental hospital is completely changed wherever the boredom of its patients' lives is changed to well-ordered work and play. Never again could I settle down to see that boredom exist."

When Dorset House was founded in 1929 it was "to enable treatment of cases of nervous disorder to be carried out on modern lines, especially with regard to the provision of adequate Occupational Therapy". The first Occupational Therapist was Miss Tebbit who had trained in America after working in mental hospitals in England. In the U.S.A. the training also included orthopaedic and general hospital experience, and with Miss Tebbit in charge the Dorset House School of Occupational Therapy was started in 1938.

An article entitled Some Experiences in Occupational Therapy by Dr Elizabeth Casson describes the work at Dorset House and its further development in Bristol:

> *For the nine years that Dorset House has been running there has been no difficulty in getting patients to fall in with a carefully arranged time table, which provides physical exercise in the form of daily Margaret Morris Movement, regular folk and ordinary dancing, walks, etc., with about two hours of craft work each day. Patients who are ready for it help with social work at nursery schools, etc., and have recreations arranged for them in the form of theatre and cinema expeditions, picnics and plenty of games at home.*

Drama was an important feature of life at Dorset House and plays were put on regularly. Elsie was fortunate in having the assistance of her nephew, Owen Reid, as a professional producer. The cast was, of course, amateur - working with enthusiasm to give pleasure to themselves as well as to the audience. Elsie and her sister Esther had often played parts in the amateur and semi-professional theatre in which her brother, Lewis Casson, built up experience. She idolised Lewis and whenever possible saw his performances. She would dress for such occasions, but was eccentric in her attire and completely oblivious to the effect she was creating. Her nephew, John Casson, tells of her arrival to join the family at the theatre in a long well-cut gown, a suitcase in one hand, a large rolled-up umbrella in the other, and, on her feet, a pair of brown, "sensible" country brogues. One of her co-workers says that she used to insist that Elsie should show herself for a last-minute check when dressed to go out. Often her hat was put on back to front. When told of this she would pull it round without even a glance in a mirror.

The picture given us of Elsie is of someone who was disciplined and dedicated in her work but who enjoyed outings and fun. A glance from her eyes "could see right into you", but it could also be humorous and kindly. She stressed the scientific nature of Occupational Therapy but had no mechanical sense - at least none when driving a car. Nevertheless countless patient' outings were carried out in a 5-seater Morris Oxford bought for £15 by Owen Reid, at Elsie's request. In this and in many other ways she was economical, having learnt the necessity of this as a girl. The profit that she was able to make at Dorset House went towards the maintenance and equipment of the Occupational Therapy School.

In addition to work at Dorset House Elsie organised a small psychiatric clinic at Bristol General Hospital and continued here until her retirement owing to ill-health in 1944. She also saw patients at the Walker Dunbar Hospital. She was active in the British Medical Association, the Medical Women's Federation and the Soroptomists, of which she was President in 1938-9.

All this would seem sufficient work for one woman but she was anxious to see Occupational Therapy developed elsewhere in Bristol. Graduated craft work was provided for rheumatic heart cases under Professor Bruce Perry at the General Hospital. Subsequently, Occupational Therapy was developed at Southmead Hospital and at Ham Green Hospital in the wards for tuberculosis.   At both these hospitals Elsie became an Honorary Consultant in Occupational Therapy. She also had the pleasure of seeing her ex-students develop the work in Bath and Warminster Hospitals.

During the 1930's Elsie gave shelter to refugees from Hitler's Germany and distinguished physicians worked as nurses for their board and lodging. Owen Reid writes "one encountered the bizarre sight of one of Freud's closest associates carrying trays up to the first floor while his wife washed up in the kitchen." By the beginning of the war in 1939 Dorset House and Mount Pleasant Clinic in Clevedon had grown to hold 100 patients. But by late 1940 Bristol became unsafe owing to the 'Blitz', and Dorset House was requisitioned, with patients transferred to two houses in Clevedon. The School of Occupational Therapy ran training courses for the Ministry of Health in an emergency hospital elsewhere and eventually was established in its present home in Oxford.

In 1948 a non-profit making Company was formed, and the following year Elsie created a trust for the benefit of Occupational Therapy including the present Dorset House. Sir Geoffrey Peto was Chairman of the Company and Elsie was Vice-Chairman and Medical Director. In 1951 two happy events took place: Elsie was awarded O.B.E in the Birthday Honours List and in July Dorset House came of age, holding an Open Day to celebrate this event. Sir Geoffrey Peto gave a welcoming speech in which he paid tribute to Elsie for her vision and effort in establishing the School.

Two years later, in December 1954, Elsie died. A Thanksgiving Service was held in July 1955 at the University Church in Oxford with Governors, staff and students and the representatives of organisations with which Elsie had been associated.

When the National Health Service was established after the war, some of Elsie's pioneering achievements were incorporated into it. She would have welcomed the use of occupational therapists into the field of assessment and support for patients in the community as well as in hospitals. Although of necessity Dorset House Clinic was a private establishment, her involvement of patients in community activities was, like so much of her work, ahead of its time. Her work is, of course, her memorial, but it would surely have given Elsie much pleasure to know that her descendants will add her name to those of her illustrious forebears.

Beryl Corner 1910 -

With the end of the Victorian era and the start of the twentieth century it might have been expected that the lot of medical women would have been relatively easy. But the career of Beryl Corner, born in 1910, who became a pioneer of neonatal medicine, shows a different picture.

Beryl was born into a Congregational family in Henleaze, Bristol, in 1910, and educated to the best standards of the day at Redland High School. Although her early promise was in science, not medicine, a visit to the school camp with a close friend, who subsequently fell ill, changed her mind. A young woman doctor, who had qualified at the Royal Free Hospital, attended her friend with such skill and tenderness that Beryl was inspired and returned home to announce to startled parents that she too would study medicine.

At the age of 17 Beryl was quickly accepted as a student by the Dean of the Royal Free Hospital in London, which could provide better training and opportunities than Bristol. Her student career echoed the success of her school life with a scholarship, bursaries and prizes, and true to the philanthropic traditions of her religious background she also helped at an East End girls' club.

After graduation most women doctors of Beryl's generation would either enter general practice or work at those maternity and child-welfare clinics described a decade later as the 'usual woman doctor's jobs'. But three months at Great Ormond street Hospital during training, coupled with a love of children, were to lead to a pioneering career as a paediatrician.

At first, beryl had a junior appointment at the Royal Free and then returned to Bristol. A consultant surgeon, also a family friend, had a vacancy for a house surgeon which he offered to Beryl. Then came a disheartening period. Further experience was essential, but each job application met with refusal. She must have had high hopes when she was short-listed for a much coveted job at the Westminster Children's Hospital. She carried out the then obligatory round of calls to the Hospital's Consultants, and knew that she had done well in the final interview. But a male candidate was appointed. She received a sympathetic letter from one of the Consultants, who confirmed that this was in spite of the fact that she 'was the best candidate by far'.

Beryl settled down to work for higher qualifications while Resident Medical Officer at the Hospital for Sick Children on St Michaels Hill. she passed the difficult examination for Membership of the Royal College of Physicians and, on the same day, heard that she had also passed the M.D. examination; both within two years of qualification, the shortest possible period in which to achieve this - an extraordinary achievement.

Before Penicillin

When Beryl qualified as a doctor in the 1930s, medical practice was atill very rudimentary. Although there were crude anaesthetics, and an understanding of the importance of sterilised enviroments at operations (and at childbirth) had established itself by now in general medical practice, there was not much else in the doctor's black bag against many of the potential killer infections and diseases. Immunisation was at a very early stage; vaccination against smallpox was compulsory and carried out by salaried public vaccinators. It was not until the 1930s that immunisation against the childhood killer, diptheria, was available. The 1950s saw the arrival of an anti-polio vaccine, and vaccines for whooping cough, measles and rubella were not widely available until the 1960s.

Children were admitted to hospital for a mixture of illnesses; gastro-enteritis was common and treated with an intravenous drip against dehydration, and to provide nourishment. A number of starved looking children suffered from coeliac disease (due to wheat intolerance, but not known then) were fed on bananas, as the food thought most easily digested. A few others might have Pink disease, due to mercury poisoning from lotions or ointments. Again, the illness disappeared as soon as the cause was identified.

There were no antibiotics such as penicillin yet. Their forerunners, the sulphonamides (named at first M and B after May and Baker who discovered them) and the German drug prontosil, were not developed until the 1930s, when they became invaluable for treating infections such as pneumonia.

Armed with her new qualifications, Beryl accepted a position at the Brompton Hospital for Diseases of the Chest in London, where she had new experience in treating a common childhood killer, T.B and T.B Meningitis. There was no antibiotic against it, and to detect T.B in a child was to pronounce a death sentence. Other children suffered T.B of the bones and joints as well as lungs, and often spent many years in long-stay hospitals, until widespread pasteurisation of milk virtually eliminated bone and joint T.B. It was only ten years later that the antibiotic drug Streptomycin was developed, and Beryl became a pioneer in its use for T.B Meningitis. Sulphonamides had preceded penicillin in the 1930s. Beryl was the first person to use the German-made 'Prontosil' to save the life of a desperately ill child in the hospital, having obtained the drug from a friend working in a London hospital. When penicillin was finally obtainable it was by injection, and surgical masks and white coats were worn when treating babies.

At about this time a post for an Honorary Physician at the Children's Hospital in Bristol became vacant. Although Beryl still lacked experience there was no likelihood of another vacancy for some time and the Consultant Surgeon who had befriended her urged her to apply. She did so knowing that at least one member of the Appointment Board opposed her and preferred a male candidate. Indeed so confident was her opponent that he did not even attend the Board meeting! To his chagrin Beryl was appointed. Her hard work and determination were at last rewarded.

Alas, there was no monetary reward. Very few doctors wanted to specialise in children's medicine in the 1930s, because it was almost impossible to make a living out of it. The study of child health and childhood diseases was hardly regarded as a discipline in its own right. In the whole of Britain there were very few paediatricians outside London, where they were rare enough. There were three or four in Birmingham and Newcastle, none at all in Bristol. There were hardly any childrens' hospitals or even childrens' wards; children were treated first by the local G.P., and then sent to mixed wards in hospital if necessary.

For Beryl to pursue her interest in children's diseases at this time, without enjoying private means, was extremely difficult, and many of her colleagues had advised her against it. Although she could live at home, Beryl still had to earn her living, and therefore a private practice was essential as there were no salaried appointments in Bristol. Until the advent of the National Health Service in 1948, the Bristol Royal Infirmary and the Bristol General Hospital were voluntary hospitals where a small number of doctors worked voluntarily for no remuneration in an honorary capacity. This system survived because it was a good way for doctors to attract the private patients that would provide their incomes, patients who would be given seperate treatment (and superior food) in the same hospital. This two-tier system of treatment was also extended to the children.

Beryl describes those years following her appointment as "five years of frustration and difficulty", as she scrambled about the South West attending lectures and conferences to increase her knowledge, and in turn giving lectures or tutorials to nurses, students, first-aiders and other fee-paying bodies, travelling to the outskirts of Bristol or to towns as far away as Swindon. Gradually she built up a private practice, making a name for herself in the field of diseases of babies and children.

Neonatal Medicine in the 1930's.

At this time, not only did the specialism of paediatrics barely exist, but also neonatal medicine was hardly heard of in the UK. Immature babies were nursed at home or in cubicles in the wards. Wrapped in cotton wool or its equivalent, the babies were fed condensed milk or a mixture of human milk and glucose water through eye droppers, and their chances of survival were minimal. During the late 1920s medical officers in Birmingham had noticed the high numbers of these low birth-weight babies (now called premature) dying at home for lack of specialist care. A

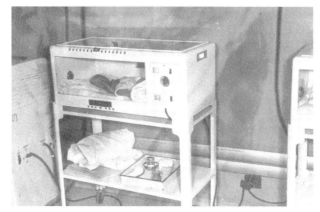

A 1949 electrically heated premature baby unit

pioneering obstetrician, Dr. Mary Cross, was appointed to set up a special care baby unit at the small Sorrento hospital. Acting on neonatal research findings from Paris, Vienna and America, Mary Cross developed the use of draught-proof deep sided cots, heated by hot water bottles (which were replenished every hour) inserted in a special cotton lining around the sides. (Electrically heated incubtors were not to arrive from America until 1949). The survival rate of tiny newborns at the Sorrento hospital began to climb.

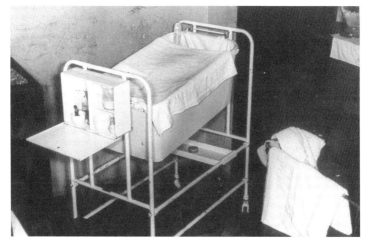

One of the first cots, heated by hot water bottles, and complete with a cupboard for baby equipment, at Southmead

Professor Parry

In 1936 a visionary man was appointed Medical Officer for Health in Bristol, Professor R.H. Parry. He immediately saw the lack of specialist children's doctors in Bristol as a scandal and in shameful contrast to the situation in much of Europe and America, where the medical branch of paediatrics had existed for decades; in Vienna even as far back as the last century. Professor Parry travelled to Chicago to review their progressive initiatives in child health, and especially in the care of new-borns. On his return, he invited Beryl to become Consultant Paediatrician to all

94

new-born babies in Corporation Hospitals and asked her to develop a service for all premature babies in the Bristol area - the first and only comprehensive service in the U.K. Despite the phenomenal work that this ground-breaking - yet barely renumerated - appointment would involve, and against all advice from her friends, Beryl accepted. She quickly introduced the Sorrento heated baby cots to Southmead, and laid the foundation of what quickly became the major centre for the treatment of low birth-weight babies in the South West.

It might have been thought that obstetric colleagues at Southmead would have welcomed a specialised paediatric service. Far from it. It is hard to say whether sex discrimination still played a part (Bristol had women Consultant Gynaecologists), whether a non-Bristol graduate was resented in a provincial environment or whether it was antagonism to a thrusting young woman upsetting the status quo. Beryl acquired a reputaion for taking on battles in all aspects of paediatric care, which she began to win by courage and quiet determination. A then junior colleague describes Beryl coming in for a hospital meal bearing what looked like shrunken bits of felt: "Babies' vests! Southmead laundry is not fit for my babies!"

The Good Family Quadruplets

Beryl was afforded one especially long-lasting pleasure as a result of the Southmead Special Baby Unit. This was the care of the Good family quadruplets in 1948, the first quads in Britain to survive after delivery by caesarean section. Paediatric care of these premature babies was followed by Beryl's involvement in the aftercare and social care for the family, aided and sponsored by the babymilk company Cow and Gate. Indeed Beryl remains a valued honorary member of the Good family to this day!

'Timothy'

A more unorthodox occupant of the early baby incubators in the 1950's was Timothy ... While Beryl was doing a ward round a colleague thrust a small bundle into her arms. "Keep it alive if you can". She unwrapped the bundle to find herself looking into the face of a tiny chimpanzee. As luck would have it an incubator and cubicle was free, and a midwife was available who had worked with the P.D.S.A. Timothy was treated like any premature baby with glucose water and human milk, changing to Carnation milk with added vitamins and iron after ten days. He thrived and after five weeks he was transferred to a specially built 'nursery' in the Zoo, at the home of the keeper and his wife. He became deeply attached to his human foster-mother and only gradually ceased crying and clinging to her as he was transferred to the parrot house with a young female chimp for company. At the age of 16 months, he was returned to his natural parents where he took the role of an affectionate nurse to younger siblings and babies. Early seperation from the mother is reported to lead to an absent sexual drive, in chimps, and attempts to introduce Timothy to a mate were failures. A home was eventually found for him in another zoo.

WWII

The advent of the Second World War and the blitz had transformed the practice of medicine in Bristol. The Children's Hospital was bombed and patients were evacuated to Weston-Super-Mare. By 1943 Beryl had to decide which of the many appointments she could accept. There was work with evacuee children outside Bristol, the Red Cross, the Emergency Service for Chest Diseases in the South West, coupled with work on a National Survey of Rickets in War-time.

On D-Day in June 1944, when the Second Front were landing in Normandy, Beryl received a phone call from the Regional Medical Officer ordering her to report at once to St. Margaret's Hospital, Swindon. No reason was given. She finished her out-patients, grabbed an over-night bag and set off. The army had requisitioned most of the hospital and she joined a group of officers, who expressed surprise at her arrival but offered her tea. They were expecting the first casualties after the Second Front. The Matron entered looking dismayed at the sight of Beryl, saying "I've no bed for a woman." Left alone, Beryl visited the wards; one was completely bare, others had trestles on which the stretchers could be placed, and others had beds. Before night fell she was joined by Mr. Ken Priddie, surgeon, his wife, and an anaesthetist. No bed was required that night as the casualties arrived, already labelled with a diagnosis and, for some of them, the letters P E N in addition. This was the first time that Beryl and her colleagues had seen the golden phials of penicillin, discovered and made in Britain but then for the sole use of the Services.

Beryl was there for three days and nights, the unwelcoming matron having eventually found her a spare cubicle in the servant's quarters, and she returned again two weeks later. This time she was billeted in a house where there was a baby and a four-year-old celebrating a birthday; sleep was limited in both places, but she had the satisfaction of assisting with 180 casualties.

The National Health Service

With the end of the war and the start of the N.H.S. came a further transformation in medicine. The struggle for money was brought to an end with a salaried service. Beryl continued with her paediatric work and became noted for clinical research, especially that of the treatment of T.B., Meningitis, jaundice and infection of the new-born. In 1947 the creation of the Department of Child Health under Professor Neale increased Beryl's work as a lecturer and member of administrative bodies and Advisory committees covering the U.K as well as Bristol. To these were added work for the British Council and World Health Organisation, and membership of scientific societies. Among these it must have given her particular pleasure to have been the first woman elected to the British Paediatric Association in 1945, President of the Medical Women's International Association in 1978-1980 and President of the Medical Women's Federation (U.K.) in 1968-1969. In addition there were, inevitably, voluntary organisations to which she gave time and energy. In Bristol in July 1996 further recognition awaited her, she was given an Honorary Bristol M.D. and joined the select group of women so honoured.

On November 29th 2000, Beryl was awarded the honorary degree of Doctor of Science by the faculty of Health and Social Care of the University of Western England (UWE):

"...in recognition of Beryl Corner's outstanding contribution to paediatric medicine and emancipation in the medical profession."

Beryl Corner receiving her honorary degree from the Chancellor of the University of Bristol 1996

4   The Entertainers

No virtuous middle class Victorian lady would have dreamed of going to the theatre. Eighteenth century Bristol women came into their own in the theatre: acting, writing plays and even running the theatres themselves: when the founder of the Jacobs Wells Theatre, John Hippisley, died, his daughter Jane Green took over as manager. Women playwrights were accepted and encouraged, even though few of their works survive or are performed today. Recently, however, there has been a successful revival, first at the Show of Strength Theatre Company and then at the Bristol Old Vic, after two hundred years of neglect, of Fanny Burney's *A Busy Day*. She had written it for Drury Lane but was interrupted by the beginnings of the French Revolution, which called Fanny's French husband home to Court.

Women singers, composers and musicians were also socially and professionally accepted during the eighteenth century, but the Victorians returned them to their drawing rooms. For women writers, the novel became a more viable artform than drama.

Silhouette of Hannah More by Augustin Edouart.

A silhouette by Augustin Edouart (1789-1861), who stated that it was a 'correct likeness of the celebrated Mrs Hannah More, taken from nature in her study at Barley Wood, the 12th June 1827.' (Reproduced by kind permission of the National Portrait Gallery, London)

Hannah More (1745 - 1833)

The changing artistic tolerances and fashions of the eighteenth and nineteenth centuries are well illustrated by the career of Hannah More, whom we have already met in Chapter 2. As if her career in philanthropy and educative reform was not enough, Hannah More was also a poet, writer, playwright and patroness of artists, admired by Dr Johnson and detested by his biographer, Boswell (and, one suspects, many other contemporaries). Her education and childhood was independent of social convention, despite the High Tory Anglicanism of her father. She was born in Fishponds in 1745, and after a rigorous early education that included French, Latin and mathematics, joined her elder sister Mary in the latter's school in Park St., which she and her sisters ran for the next thirty years.

Hannah enjoyed teaching, and enhanced her classes by writing tales and verses for her pupils, and dramatising Bible stories for their enjoyment and edification. Her own interest in drama began early at the age of 16 when she wrote an improving yet lively pastoral drama for her pupils, *The Search after Happiness*. It was published in 1773 and went into nine editions, selling 10,000 copies, so suitable was its message that educated women could still be good wives and mothers. The following year another play, *The Inflexible Captive*, was staged at the Bath Theatre Royal. The Theatre Royal opened in Bristol in 1776, and Hannah certainly saw no reason why her schoolgirls should not be taken there.

Hannah's interest in the theatre had been enthusiastically encouraged by her new circle of London friends, to whom she had been introduced when, accompanied by her sisters Sally and Patty, Hannah visited London for the first time in 1774. Hannah met a number of influential literary and artistic Londoners, including Sir Joshua Reynolds and the great Dr Johnson: with the latter there developed a long-lasting friendship in spite of the difference in their ages. Even more important to her was the meeting with the actor-manager and dramatist, David Garrick and his Austrian wife, Eva. (Garrick had been a pupil of Johnson). Hannah was enthralled by Garrick's performances and soon became an intimate friend of David and Eva, staying at their home, and the experience directly or indirectly inspired her to become a dramatist herself. Garrick's nickname for Hannah was 'Nine', as in muses, because she was proficient in all the arts.

Two years after the success of *The Inflexible Captive*, *Percy*, a raging melodrama in five acts about the Border feud between the great houses of Percy and Douglas, was put on successfully at the Theatre Royal, Drury Lane. The plot, in which the heroine, Elwina, is forced to marry the enemy of her own true love, was reputed to make strong men weep. It ran for two months at Drury Lane and was still being staged in Bath and Bristol up to 1815, earning Hannah £600 in royalties.

Hannah wrote one more play, *The Fatal Falsehood*, in 1778, which again was approved by Garrick and was performed by Sarah Siddons in Bath. Garrick died shortly afterwards, in 1779, and by this stage Hannah was discovering a more serious purpose in life. She renounced the theatre for good, saying it was inimical to Christianity. We have already explored Hannah's subsequent career as a moral improver and educator in Chapter 2; and in Chapter 5 we shall meet her yet again as a partroness of the arts.

Sarah Siddons (1755 - 1831)

Bristol had a long theatrical tradition. The Jacobs Wells Theatre opened in 1729, to be replaced by the Theatre Royal in 1766 which has been in continuous use ever since, was bound to adopt its favourite actresses.

The most famous English actress of the day was Sarah Siddons. She really belongs to Bath, but she often worked in Bristol, taking lodgings in Princes Buildings, and appearing in all the great roles - including Hamlet - at both the Bristol and the Bath theatres, between 1775 and 1782. She was paid the top salary of £3 a week and earned every penny: "Hard labour indeed it was," she wrote, " for after the rehearsal at Bath on a Monday morning I had to go and act at Bristol in the evening of the same day....a drive of twelve miles."

Sarah had such a forceful personality that her ghost is still supposed to haunt both the Bristol and Bath Theatres Royal. She was not so much loved as admired and lionised by her public. Hannah More was most impressed by her powers and invited her to "declaim" at her home, Barley Wood, in the presence of De Quincy; Sir Thomas Lawrence the Bristol-born painter did her full-length portrait in a dramatic pose. (He also paid court to her two daughters in succession). One of these daughters subsequently died at the Hotwell, one of the many consumptive patients that the spa water could not save.

Mary Robinson (1758 - 1800)

Known as the English Sappho, Mary Robinson was another Bristol actress of great popularity. She was the daughter of a Bristol whale merchant, and was educated at the More school in Park Street, but left when her father lost his money and ran off with his mistress. Mary was hastily married off at 16 to a Bristol solicitor called Robinson, but this marriage failed when she, her husband and small daughter were thrown for a brief period into a debtor's prison. On her release Mary was left to bring up her daughter alone.

Gainsborough's portrait of Mary Robinson as 'Perdita'

She managed it by going on the stage, and won renown for her beauty and intelligence, as well as for her acting. Her success as Perdita, in The Winter's Tale, was such that she became the mistress of the 18 year old Prince Regent, later George IV. The Prince lavished money on her, and she became the toast of high society. Her fashions were imitated, Romney and Gainsborough painted her. The demands of being a Royal Mistress were such that Mary had to give up the stage, but the King lost patience with bawdy public satires about the Prince's scandalous philandering, and forced the affair to a close. Mary was apparently owed £20,000 by the Prince, which was never repaid.

Ever-resourceful, she took on the alias of Tabitha Bramble and wrote novels and poems, moving Coleridge to acclaimher as an "undoubted genius". Mary's star rose again and she even visited Paris as the guest of Marie Antoinette. Nonetheless she died penniless and deserted in 1800, aged only 42.

The Terry Sisters
Kate Terry (1844 - 1924), Dame Ellen Terry (1848 - 1928)

Almost a century later, the two most famous entertainers in late Victorian England both had their apprenticeships in Bristol: the classical actress Ellen Terry and singer Clara Butt. Both became national idols and finally Dames of the British Empire. They were the unsurpassed stars of their day.

The beautiful Kate Terry and her younger sister Ellen were hired for the 1862 season by James Chute, manager of Bristol's Theatre Royal, where a century earlier another visiting actress, Sarah Siddons, had been made an honorary Bristolian. Ellen was only 14 but already an experienced actress, for she had been born into a theatrical family that two generations later was to produce the great actor John Gielgud.

Kate was engaged as the leading lady, to play tragic roles like Marguerite in Faust, and Ophelia in Hamlet, while Ellen played the mischievous juvenile roles like Cupid and Puck. She had to turn her hand to every-thing and was disconcerted to find that she had to play in burlesque - comical caricatures of serious works or subjects - as part of her duties as a utility member of a stock company.

In her highly selective memoirs, The ***Story of My life***, Ellen wrote: *"I told the stage manager I couldn't sing and I couldn't dance. His reply was short and to the point. 'You've got to do it.' And so I did it in a way - very funny way at first, no doubt.... it was admirable training for it took all the self-consciousness out of me to start with. To end with I thought it capital fun and enjoyed burlesque as much as Shakespeare."*

The enchanting sisters had lodgings in Queen Square nearby and were so haunted by their admirers that they had to be chaperoned to the theatre every day A shop-boy was so infatuated by Kate that he embezzled his firm's money in order to buy her expensive presents. Ellen remembered "My mother was most vigilant in her role as duenna from the time I first went on the stage until I was a grown woman. I can never remember going home unaccompanied by her or my father."

At the end of their 1862 season the sisters composed a Valedictory Address which was printed on silk and sold to the audience. It was called The Two Homes and was a graceful doggerel tribute to Bristol:

> *Henceforth we'll call this place our other Home*
> *and trust (tho' life uncertain be and short)*
> *that we again and yet again may come,*
> *'Ere we grow old, and be Laid up in Port.*
> *Goodbye then, till we meet again - come Nell,*
> *and bid with me - our Bristol friends farewell.*

They did return for the 1863 season and at the end of this had a joint benefit night (when they had a share of the takings) Kate also received a gold bracelet set with a horseshoe of pearls and a pretty gold pencil case with a letter from an admiring chemist... For their farewell perform-ances, they played Portia and Nerissa in **The Merchant of Venice**, and Beatrice and Hero in **Much Ado About Nothing**.

The pair returned again in 1867 and the **Clifton Chronicle** theatre corre-spondent wrote "the whole city has been wild about them during the past two weeks, despite the wretched melodrama in which they played and a heavy blizzard blocking the traffic."   Another star at the time was Henrietta Hodson, who took soubrette roles and rival factions, the Hodsonites and the Terryites, were formed! Ellen later praised the basic training she received in Bristol, calling it:

The experience of my life.... There was no question of parts suiting us;
we had to take what we were given ... as part of a company that was
more than sound." She liked all the praise too. "We were petted,
spoiled and applauded to our heart's content and I don't think it did
us any harm. We all had scores of admirers but their youthful ardour
seemed to be satisfied by tracking us when we went to rehearsal in the
morning and meeting us outside the stage door at night.

It was during her Bristol Theatre Royal days that Ellen, still a teenager, met the Bristol architect Edward Godwin, who lived in style at 21 Portland Square. He was a keen archaeologist and had written a book, *The Architectural Antiquities of Bristol.*

He designed a few of Bristol's more interesting Victorian buildings, like the now derelict carriage works in Stokes Croft, 10 and 11 Rockleaze, Sneyd Park, Westbury-on-Trym parish rooms, and part of the Bristol Royal Infirmiry; nationally he became famous for his neo-Gothic designs for the Northampton Town Hall. Godwin also loved the theatre, and was Secretary of the Bristol Shakespeare Society, and the Terrys went to some of his Shakespeare readings. As theatre critic for the Western Daily Press he started heated debates in Bristol on the standard of work in the city's theatre, and in return his opponents attacked his buildings.

Ellen Terry as Ophelia

Godwin also designed stage costumes, and when Chute took his company to the Bath Theatre Royal in 1863, he made the Titania costume and headdress for Ellen, who visited his house for a fitting.

"This house, with its Persian rugs, beautiful furniture, its sense of design in every detail, was a revelation to me, and the talk of its master and mistress made me think. At the theatre I was living in an atmosphere which was developing my powers as an actress and teaching me what work meant, but my mind had begun to grasp dimly and almost unconsciously that I must do something for myself - something that all my education and training I was receiving in my profession could not do for me."

Godwin taught the young Ellen about clothes. For the Titania dress, which was daringly clinging, "he showed me how to damp it and wring it while it was wet, tying up the material as the Orientals do in their tie and dry process so that when it was dried and untied, it was all crinkled and clinging. It was the first lovely dress I ever wore and I learned a great deal from it."

What Ellen Terry does not mention in *The Story Of My Life* is that a few years later on, Godwin, then aged 35, became her lover. She married the artist George Frederick Watts in 1865; she was 16 and he was 46, and there is doubt that the marriage was ever consummated. In London she met the by now widowed Godwin again and caused a minor scandal by going to nurse him when he was ill, and staying the night. This was pretext enough for Watts to disown her and Ellen and Godwin eloped.

For the years 1868-1874, the young actress went missing from the stage completely, and no-one knew where she was. In fact she was living with Godwin in Hertfordshire and enjoying a rural idyll. "I studied cookery books instead of parts - Mrs. Beeton instead of Shakespeare!".

Godwin fathered her two sons Ted and Eddy Craig, and in the village she called herself Mrs. Godwin. As an architect Godwin burned out early and this disappointment, as well as financial worries, made the relationship turn sour after the birth of the children.

An accident with a pony and trap led to a chance meeting with the actor manager Charles Reade, who promptly offered Ellen £40 a week to come back to the stage. She agreed, and made her comeback in 1874 and went on acting until her death in 1928.

She and Godwin lived uncomfortably together in Bloomsbury, until he abandoned her in 1875, having started a relationship with a young trainee architect Beatrice Phillips, who eventually became his second wife. In 1877 Watts finally divorced Ellen for adultery with Godwin. She never married again, and her son always claimed that Godwin was the love of her life. Not one word of this emotional turmoil is mentioned in The Story of My Life.

In later years Ellen often appeared on stage with another Bristol actor, Sir Henry Irving. Rumour had it that they too were lovers. She certainly was the great love of George Bernard Shaw's life, and was beloved and admired by all up to her death in 1928.

Clara Butt (1873 - 1936)

Not a single whiff of scandal can be attached to Bristol's other great artistic treasure, Dame Clara Butt, who became a national institution, rather like the Queen. "There is nature... there is Art... and there is Clara Butt" proclaimed the actor manager Sir Herbert Tree.

Clara was not born in the city but came to live at 3, Sydney Terrace, Totterdown, with her parents Clara and Henry (another pair of elopers) in 1880, when she was seven. Her father was a sea captain who in Bristol ventured into shipbuilding and lost all his money when his schooner *Crystal* was sunk with all hands.

The family went through a bad patch, but was able to send the young Clara to the Bath Road Academy. She had her first music lessons from Miss Adelaide Fincken, but though she soon became proficient, she was not keen on the piano, though she did acquire a taste for hymns.

Clara Butt

Her mother was a fine singer, and singing came naturally to her daughter, so it was suggested that Clara have singing lessons as well. The family had moved to Mida Villa in Coronation Road and next door was a teacher of singing, a Mrs. Brooks, who being a soprano, concluded that Clara was as well. But after attending a concert at the Colston Hall to hear the contralto Belle Cole, Clara tried to imitate the sound she had heard, and found that she could sing comfortably in that register as well. She would boom away in the parlour and see if passers by in the street could hear her.

When Clara was a twelve year old pupil at South Bristol High School the head mistress persuaded the leading singing teacher in Bristol, Dan Rootham, to listen to her. The rest is history. Rootham famously proclaimed "You have gold in your throat, my child" and Clara's career began, slowly at first, with a place with the Bristol Festival Chorus, then solo oratorio work, and song recitals in chapels and mission halls for temperance meetings and Bible classes. She was proud to earn a little money to prop up the ailing family finances, and jubilant when she earned two guineas singing at the Bristol Saturday Pops, which were concerts of popular music - 'lollipops'.

It was at this stage that she met her accompanist Miss Alice Jenkins, who described her as "a tall girl, all arms and legs, with a rather unmanageable voice." Clara could fill a room to the point of discomfort with her extraordinary dramatic renderings of such popular works as *The Enchantress*.

In 1887, when she was 16, her teacher Daniel Rootham entered her for the preliminary Royal College of Music examination, and despite the fact that organist George Riseley, Rootham's arch-rival, was adjudicator, Clara passed and was entered for the final examination in London. This meant she could win a place at the Royal College and train professionally.
It was her first visit to the capital. Despite her terror, for her audition she plunged into a passionate rendering of *The Enchantress*. The judges stared, jumped to their feet, waved their arms, walked about talking, and Clara sang louder and louder, getting angry because she thought they were laughing at her.

In fact the judges were stunned by the astounding voice they were hearing. "I knew that even in its immature state it was the most beautiful contralto voice I had ever heard in all my long experience" said one of the judges afterwards. They asked her to sing something quieter and she sang *Woe Unto Them* from Handel's Elijah, and the College place was hers.

There was huge excitement in Bristol when the time came for her to leave in 1890. Her friends arranged a farewell concert in her honour and collected two purses of gold, one of which contained a cheque for £601. It could have been the end of her connection with Bristol, but her family still lived there, and Clara's gratitude to the city which launched her never failed, even when she became world famous.

Soon Bristol was basking in reflected glory, for the young music student was discovered by the Princess of Wales, who asked her to sing whenever they met, even if it was in a shop in Baker Street. She started to sing solos for the Royal Choral Society, and though the Royal College of Music's rule was that students could only perform in their final year, they made an exception so that she could earn some pocket money, and send funds home to Bristol.

Clara made her professional debut at the Albert Hall, singing in Gluck's *Orpheus*. The music critics were amazed; soon word got round London that this 6ft 2ins tall 19 year-old singer was sensational. Queen Victoria asked Clara to sing at Buckingham Palace, and then at Windsor, and Ellen Terry and Sir Henry Irving and Sir Arthur Sullivan came to her concerts. Even at this early stage, she had offers from America.

In 1891, when Clara was living at Hyde Park Mansions in London, a composer who called with some songs to show her was told to come back the next day, because she was in the bath. The caller was Edward Elgar and the songs he wanted her to look at were the **Sea Pictures**. She gave the first performance of the song cycle at Norwich in 1899.

Elgar also wrote the part of the Angel in **The Dream Of Gerontius** with Clara in mind, and Land of Hope and Glory was actually written at her suggestion. Sir Arthur Sullivan wrote **The Lost Chord** for her, and her fellow student Samuel Liddle arranged for her what was to become her signature tune, **Abide With Me**, which she had to sing at every concert; her recording of Liddle's arrangement became the favourite at the Front during World War 1, and now of course it has been adopted on the football terraces.

With her future secure at an amazingly early age, Clara did not forget Bristol before embarking on an international career: she played a flying visit to open a bazaar and in 1893 sang at the Bristol Festival at the Colston Hall, before dashing to Paris to sing Handel's **Delilah** for Saint-Saens himself. Everywhere she went she was feted; in Berlin a wealthy suitor kept sending her jewels, in Budapest admirers hired bands to serenade her wherever she went. When she fell from her horse and lay unconscious under a hedge for two hours before being rescued, she had shoals of get well telegrams, including one from Queen Victoria.

Canada welcomed her on tour in 1899 with the same enthusiasm and on the same circuit was a bass baritone, Robert Kennerley Rumford. The pair sang duets and he would pencil little messages of love in German on her score, and this was the way he proposed, during a rendition of **The Keys of Heaven.**

There was as much fuss in the press as for a royal engagement, and Clara was offered a great honour, the chance to get married in St. Paul's Cathedral. But she turned it down, saying she wanted to get married in Bristol. For the first time in a century, a wedding was to take place in Bristol Cathedral, on June 26, 1900. Every major newspaper sent a reporter to fill pages of print on the wedding of the year.

It was as good as a royal wedding, for everyone had the day off and what seemed like the entire city turned out to honour her. Special trains from London were laid on, church bells were rung, and the streets were packed from dawn. The city itself presented Clara with a diamond brooch with the initials CB, City of Bristol, or Clara Butt, transfixed by a ruby arrow; it was one among hundreds of wedding gifts including one from the Queen herself. (The brooch was eventually donated to the city by Dame Clara's daughter and is now in the City Museum).

There was a minor riot when the cathedral was opened to fill the remaining places after the 500 official guests had been allowed in; among them were Madame Albani, Belle Cole, Nellie Melba, and Forbes Robertson, and many well-known singers sat in the choir stalls and joined in the hymns. Sir Arthur Sullivan, who was to have played the organ, but was ill, composed a special Wedding Anthem, ***O God Thou Art Worthy To Be Praised.***

Clara wore a dress in heavy cream crepe de chine trimmed with matching silk fringe and her sisters were bridesmaids; one of her pages was a little lad called Ivor Novello. It was on her wedding day that she paid off the last £600 of her father's overdraft and settled other family debts to the tune of several hundred pounds. In twelve years, Clara had gone from almost rags to great riches.

The newly weds became a dream couple; they always performed together, they had three children, a seaside home and an imposing mansion in Hampstead, where they kept exotic pets - Clara liked parrots. They willingly went on endless national and international tours, always making sure that Bristol was on the itinerary.

Clara evidently had a showbiz streak in her that led her to design spectacular dresses for her public appearances. She had everything named after her from racehorses to soap, perfumes and ice creams, and she was constantly deluged with fanmail. She also loved practical jokes and would hoax people on the telephone, by pretending to be a man.

She was not averse to endorsing musical products either. "I feel that you have in this invention easily placed the Grafonola several years in advance of any other known gramophone," went the advertisement for the New Columbia Grafonola. She also got a hefty fee for saying that the Schieelmayer piano "was such a help to the voice", and she lent her approval to sheet music as well.

It is hard to judge what her voice was really like, because the popular image of her is the foghorn voice we hear in the old recording of ***Land Of Hope And Glory***. Dame Clara refused to make any recordings at all until 1909, and the repertoire she sang was ephemeral. But a surviving recording of her singing the Angel in Elgar's ***Gerontius*** reveals a much more subtle voice of rich tonal colouring, capable of singing a thrilling pianissimo. So eager were the record companies to buy her services that the Gramophone Company set up a recording studio in her own home, so that she would not have to travel.

Her choice of music did not shy away from the popular: at her Grand Concert To Say Goodbye (she was off to Australia and new Zealand) she sang for her Bristol fans ***Break, Break, Break***, ***Abide With Me***, ***My Own***

Land, *My Dear Zoul*, (a Wessex lovesong), ***Believe Me If All Those Endearing Young Charms***; on her return, the audience at the Colston Hall in June 1908 heard ***The Lost Chord***, Handel's ***Largo***, and ***The Day Is Done***.

Nor did her repertoire develop much, for at the Colston Hall concert in January, 1924, (the programme said "No artist has a greater hold on the Bristol public than this wonderful Queen of Song") she was still singing the pops, and rarely performed any lieder, or operatic arias, preferring the old favourites that her fans loved, now forgotten numbers like ***I Know My Love***, ***So Little Time***, ***A Song of Comfor***t and ***The Beautiful Land of Nod***:

> *Come cuddle your head on my shoulder, dear,*
> *your head like the golden rod,*
> *And we'll go sailing away from here*
> *to the beautiful land of Nod.*

She did sing the odd song by Debussy or Brahms or Chausson but the general tone was light and undemanding, with the odd dash of drama thrown in :

> *Women of Inver, tis straight ye stand,*
> *full ankle deep in the shifting sands,*
> *Your eyes on the sea and your backs to the land,*
> *when the fishing fleet sets sail.*

Dame Clara - she was made a Dame in 1920 - somehow symbolised the Empire and the Monarchy and the British spirit and she played up to this image, with her special arrangement of the national anthem, recorded with the Band of the Coldstream Guards, who clearly came second in the contest, and her Coronation anthem of 1911, which praised Great Britain:

> *Glory be with her and peace evermore.*
> *Purest! Surest!*
> *Royal! Loyal!*
> *God bless our Empire for now and for aye!*

She worked tirelessly for the war effort from 1914 -18, and supported women artists and founded the Three Arts Women's Unemployment Fund; she gave generously to charity and never forgot her Bristol links, but perhaps this magnificent voice was not fully used in any serious way. She died, a very wealthy woman, in 1936 and was genuinely mourned by the musical world, and by her loyal fans in Bristol. It had truly been a voice of gold.

Eva Turner (1892 - 1990)

Another musical dame was taught by Clara Butt's teacher, Daniel Rootham. Eva Turner was born in Oldham in 1892, but grew up in Bristol, a city to which she constantly returned in later life, to attend Welsh National Opera productions at the Bristol Hippodrome. As with Clara, Rootham trained her for a musical scholarship at the Royal Academy, where she studied from 1911 to 1915. She was inspired to become an opera singer after hearing the Carl Rosa company perform in Bristol, and she herself became a chorus member in 1915.

Eva made her solo debut at the page in Tannhauser in 1916, and soon moved onto major soprano roles such as Santuzza, Tosca, Aida and *Madame Butterfly*. As with Clara, her voice was spotted by Ettone Paurezza, who sent her to Milan to sing for Toscanini. she made her debut at *La Scala* in Milan as Freia in 1924, and became the leading dramatic soprano of the company. Two years later she sang the title role of the first performance of *Turandot*, the role with which she is most associated. Alfaro, who completed the unfinished Puccini opera, considered that she was ideal for the role. The old recordings still retain glimmerings of how moving and powerful her performances could be.

Her voice was steady right through its range, and she could produce a seamless legato. Her diction was faultless, and although she was very small in stature, she had a tremendous dramatic presence. It was said that her Wagnerian high C could be heard in the street outside Covent Garden!

Eva sang at Covent Garden for several seasons up to the war, which she spent performing concerts for the forces. She stayed with the Royal Opera until 1949, when she began a teaching career at the University of Oklahoma, and later at the Royal Academy. Gwynneth Jones was one of her pupils.

In 1962 Eva was made a Dame. She died in 1990, aged 97, living long enough to see all her recordings re-issued on CD. She left Bristol a strange little legacy: the one sure test of whether someone is a Bristolian or not is to make them say: "Dame Eva Turner, prima donna of the Carl Rosa Opera Company" without inserting a hint of an 'l' at the end of any word.

Ruby Helder (1890 - 1938)

Ruby Helder's claim to musical fame is unique - she was the only female professional tenor ever.

She was born Emma Jane Holder, in 1890, and brought up in a pub called the Glasshouse in Lawrence Hill, Bristol, where her father was the landlord. That is where she would practice. She so astounded the regulars that she was encouraged to have proper singing lessons, and went on to train at the Guildhall in London, as a baritone in those days, not even a tenor! Since another student already there had the same surname, she changed hers to Helder.

Ruby had her first break thanks to her aunt, who was the housekeeper of Sir Harry Lauder, a popular Scottish singer, who had the right contacts to help her make her professional debut at the Queen's Hall in London, in 1909. Four years later she was already commanding £10,000 a performance, a most extraordinary sum for the time. Thanks to her unique voice - she had the same power and range as male tenors - she went on to sing around the world, after the great Italian tenor Enrico Caruso brought her to the public's notice. He was amazed that her two-octave vocal range was only three notes short of his own.

Ruby's repertoire was not grand opera - as the casting might have been confusing for the audience - but rather popular favourites of the day such as *Be Thou Faithful*, *Good Night Beloved*, *Songs of Araby* and *Come into the Garden, Maud*. She made several recordings, which have since been re-issued on CD, as a curiosity (Ruby Helder, Girl Tenor by Pearl Records GEMMCD1). Ruby married an American artist and emigrated to the United States in 1933, and retired from concert-giving three years later. She died in Hollywood in 1938, aged only 48.

5 Writers and Artists

S A R A H   *F A R L E Y's*

BRISTOL JOURNAL.

Printed by WILLIAM ROUTH,   No. 18, in *BRIDGE-STREET*.

VOLUME LXXXI.   SATURDAY, JULY 2, 1796.   No. 4175 {WEEKS SINCE THIS JOURNAL WAS FIRST PUBLISHED.

There had been a strong tradition of writing and publishing by Bristol women, even well before the 19th century. Many of them, now totally forgotten, were nevertheless best sellers in their day, such as the 17th century Mary Dudley, Quaker preacher and biographer, and her fellow Quaker and pamphleteer, Sarah Jones, or school mistress Anne Raikes Harding, who in 1818 published anonymously seven novels of strong Christian content. Mary Bryan, wife of a Bristol printer and bookseller, had to wait until she became a widow in 1845, before she could issue the poems her husband had forbidden her to publish. Mary ran the printing business herself for some years, and this was not uncommon in Bristol, a printing city.

In the 18th century, for some years both the major Bristol newspapers were owned and run by women. When brothers Felix and Samuel Farley both died in 1753, Elizabeth, Felix's widow, took over one Bristol Journal, and Samuel's niece Sarah, the other. When she died in 1774 the newspaper was sold to William Routh, be to taken over by his widow Catherine when he died.

Another rebel was Frances Norton, wife of Sir George Norton of Abbot's Leigh, an essayist and poet who in 1714 published in Bristol a Miscellany of her poems written, she said dryly, "to embroider on chairbacks." She said, "Unhappy marriage is to tear each other's flesh and gnaw their bones."

The poems and essays of Southey's wife Caroline Bowles were eclipsed by her husband's fame, and also forgotten are sisters Harriet and Sophia Lee, dramatists who lived from the 1750s to the 1820s. They had some practical knowledge of the theatre, for their father John had managed the Theatre Royal at Bath and the two girls did the same at one stage. Their writing had a Gothic feminist tinge and at least they wrote comedies, with titles like **The Errors of Innocence**, **The Mysterious Marriage** and **The New Peerage**. One of their best successes on stage was **A Chapter of Accidents**, and they made enough money from this play to open a school.

The Porter Sisters (1776 - 1850)

Another related pair of writers were sisters Jane and Anna Maria Porter, who lived from 1776-1850, and wrote over 30 works, most of them historical romances. Their most famous work was published in 1803. Thaddeus of Warsaw was a true story of Polish patriot and exile Thaddeus Kosciuszko who came to visit Bristol in 1797 and stayed at 37 Queen Square. He fought in Washington's army and then returned to Poland to fight for liberty against first the Russians and then the Prussians, eventually ending up in a St. Petersburg prison.

The Porter sisters, who lived in Portland Square, were avid readers, and were inspired by tales of daring and chivalry they heard from a boy called Walter Scott, who came to stay at their house. Later one of Jane's best sellers was Scottish Chiefs, in five volumes, a book which Scott later acknowledged as the inspiration for the Waverley novels. Another favourite with the public was a diary of a family shipwrecked on a desert island - was Sir Edward Seaward's Narrative genuine or not?

Anne Yearsley: the Milkmaid Poet (1752-1806)

Ann Yearsley was unwise enough to engage in unequal combat with Hannah More, her patron. It is not an edifying story, for More was high-handed and Yearsley was ungrateful, and the scandal has obscured the question that really matters: was she any good as a poet?

The facts of the case are well-known: More discovered Ann Yearsley, a milkmaid, and her family living in dire poverty, and hearing that the uneducated woman had a talent for poetry, she undertook to get a collection of her verses published. She went to considerable trouble to find 1,000 subscribers, from bishops and duchesses to poets and novelists among her literary and society friends to produce a volume - with errors of grammar corrected - in 1785. It was a large, handsome, leather-bound volume called ***Poems On Several Occasions by Ann Yearsley, a Milkwoman of Bristol***. The Bluestockings christened her Lactilla.

In the preface Hannah More describes how in winter of 1783 she discovered the unlettered muse. She had ordered kitchen scraps to be given to the family, to feed their pig. The family was destitute, with five children to feed and a sixth on the way; the landlord had taken the cows and the famished husband sat by the hearth of his stripped cottage; old mother lay bedridden in a corner on a heap of straw and the children crying for food.

> *A copy of verses was shown to me, said to be written by a poor illiterate woman in this neighbourhood, who sells milk door to door. The story did not engage my faith but the verses excited my attention, for, though incorrect, they breathed the genuine spirit of Poetry, and were rendered more interesting, by a certain natural and strong expression of misery which seemed to fill the heart and mind of the author.... I found she had been born and bred in her present humble station and had never received the least education except that her brother had taught her to read...*
> *She is about eight and twenty, was married very young to a man who is said to be honest and sober, but of a turn of mind very different from her own... when I went to see her I observed a perfect simplicity in her manner without the least affectation or pretension of any kind... and her remarks on the books she had read are so accurate and so consonant with the opinions of the best critics.*

The novelist Fanny Burney, who knew the Clifton and Hotwells social scene well, having visited and set her novel ***Evelina*** there, met the literary curiosity and described her to Dr. Johnson: "She is plain but not disagreeable to look at and has a good singing voice."

What Yearsley had read was the Bible, Shakespeare, Pope, Young, and some classical translations, and she would read prints and pamphlets displayed in booksellers' windows. Hannah More gave her a dictionary and a grammar, and the result was a highly competent imitation of the high-flown 18th century verse style, full of abstractions and lofty sentiment.

The verses are elegant and gloomy, mainly over her own miserable state, and there is hardly an individual poetic voice to be heard. As Bristol's poet laureate Robert Southey wrote, in his ***Lives Of The Unlettered Poets***, "Though gifted with voice she had no strain of her own whereby to be remembered, but she was no mocking bird...Many of the poems are about her own situation, that of a 'Genius Unimproved.'":

Dauntless thought I eagerly seized, no formal rule e're awed;
No precedent controlled; no custom fixed my independent spirit:
On the wing she still shall guideless soar.

Even on her task as a milkmaid she overdoes it:

Lactilla, shivering tends her fav'rite cow,
The bleating flocks now ask the bounteous hand
And Crystal streams in frozen fetters stand.

On Bristol's slave trade:

Bristol! Thy heart hath throbbed to glory,
Slaves, e'een Christian slaves have shook their chains
And gazed with wonder and amazement on thee.

When she tried for a lighter note, the effect was clumsy yet hilarious:

On the axis of Love wheels the Universe round,
In rotation continued and thrifty,
While some tender minds at 15 feel the wound,
And some hold it out till they're fifty.

Better is this poem about the return of a merchant ship coming up the Avon Gorge:

Joy tunes the cry; the rocks rebound the roar,
The deep vibration quivers long the shore,
The merchant hears and hails the peeping mast,
The wave-drenched sailor scorns all perils past;
Now love and joy the noisy crews invite,
And clumsy music crowns the rough delight.

Because of the influential patrons, the volume sold well and the first edition produced around £350, then a fair sum, which Hannah More proceeded to put in trust for the family. At the end of the year More invited Yearsley to her house, but when the poetess asked for a copy of the deed of trust, More is supposed to have said: "Are you mad Mrs. Yearsley, or have you drunk a glass too much? Who are your advisors? I am certain you have drank, or you would not talk to me in this manner! " Miss More's friends claimed that the milkmaid had then thrown the money at her patron's head. The quarrel was a nine days wonder in London, but caused a prolonged feud in Bristol.

The dispute really arose because Ann Yearsley wanted to jointly administer the funds herself - chiefly she wanted the cash to pay for her son's education. More accused her of ingratitude, and according to some reports, the two almost came to blows. "I felt as a mother deemed unworthy the tuition or care of her family" wrote Yearsley of the quarrel in her Vindication.

The resentment smouldered on and Yearsley pointedly paid for the 'dish-washings' collected from More's kitchen, to feed her cow. She also hit back in print, saying that More had treated her to "insulting ungracious admonitions" and had burned her original manuscript. The collision was almost inevitable, as true communication between the high-minded and patronising bluestocking and the ungrateful peasant with a chip on her shoulder and ideas above her station was almost impossible.

With the best of motives, More feared that Yearsley would go on a spending spree, or would foolishly imagine that she could make a living from her writing. " I hope she is convinced that the making of verses is not the great business of human life and that as a wife and mother she has duties to fill, the smallest of which is of more value than the finest verses she can write," wrote the spinster More, who was just 40 at the time, and continued mournfully "Had she turned out well, I should have had my reward; as it is I have my trial... poor human nature, I could weep over thee. Nothing but the sanctifying influence of religion can subdue and keep in tolerable order that pride which is the concomitant of great talents with a bad education."

The argument was eventually resolved by handing the money over to a Bristol merchant, who handed on the hot potato to Yearsley, to open a circulating library in the Colonnade at Hotwells. More had scorned this idea, because most libraries of the day were full of foolish escapist fantasies for girls.

More was then able to organise the indignation of the establishment, who turned on the poor milkmaid. Maria Edgeworth wrote in a letter of 1791 from her home in Princes Buildings, Clifton: "Mrs. Yearsley the milkmaid lives very near us; we have never seen her and probably never shall, for my father is so indignant against her for her ingratitude to her benefactor Miss Hannah More, that he thinks she deserves to be treated with neglect. She was dying, absolutely expiring with hunger when Miss More found her." Horace Walpole nastily said that the milkmaid's verses had been "washed and comb'd" by Miss More, but her Bristol publisher and friend of the poets Coleridge and Wordsworth had more sympathy and said she had "an angry dignity."

Yearsley went on to produce further literary efforts, including a play, **Earl Godwin**, which was actually performed at the Theatre Royal in Bristol and Bath in 1789, though it had very few performances.

Another work was ***The Royal Captive***, a Gothic tale of prisoners and oppression of women, and altogether she published ten volumes, though none of them brought the financial rewards of the first. Her work was instantly forgotten, probably quite rightly, and only the record of the famous row with Hannah More remains. Yearsley died, still obsessed with her wrongs, at Melksham in 1806.

As for Hannah More's own literary achievements, they too have not stood the test of time, for to modern taste they are too pedantic, humourless and obviously didactic. She was certainly scholarly and amazingly prolific, but all her writings have designs on people - who else could have written ***Stories for Persons of the Middle Rank*** or ***Twenty-One long chapters on Practical Piety?***

A taste of the earnest style to come was already evident in the Search After Happiness, a Pastoral Drama for Young Ladies, written when she was 15 for the Park Street schoolgirls to perform:

> *While Beauty and Pleasure are now in their prime,*
> *And Folly and Fashion expect our whole time,*
> *Ah! Let not these phantoms our wishes engage;*
> *Let us live so in youth, that we blush not in age.*

Women Explorers and Travel Writers

Travel abroad and writing were two trades that educated Victorian woman of means could turn to without fear of social ostracism. The combination of plucky Englishwomen writing about their travel experiences in heathen territories was irresistible to the public. During the nineteenth century a trickle of colourful memoirs, tracts and papers swelled to a flood, which thrilled the imaginations of readers as much as the most ardent confections of the nineteenth century novelists, and fuelled the passion for travel and exploration.

Anna Maria Falconbridge (fl. 1791 -3)

The precedent had already been set a century before by aristocratic Englishwomen of means to travel widely and independently. One of the earliest intrepid women from Bristol was Anna Maria Falconbridge, who in 1791 married against family wishes and went with her husband Alexander, a surgeon, to the African colony of Sierra Leone, in order to rescue a number of stranded colonists. In those pre-abolition days Falconbridge was hardly a popular figure in Bristol, for he had written an exposé of the slave trade.

The pair went to Africa to help re-organise the newly acquired colony, and Anna Maria sent home letters which she obviously meant for publication, such is their tone and content. She set out to describe *"the Distresses and proceedings of the settlement with a description of the Manners, Diversions, Arts, Commerce, Cultivation, Customs, Punishments etc., and Every Interesting Particular relating to the Sierra Leone colony and also the present State of the Slave Trade in the West Indies and the Improbability of its total abolition."*

She was not violently opposed to slavery, but in the colony became indignant on behalf of the British women who had been kidnapped in London's East End and brought out to be used as prostitutes by the colonists. Her letters, published in 1794 as **A Narrative of Two Voyages To The River Sierra Leone 1791-93**, and dedicated to the people of Bristol, also remarked on the hard labour of the native women and the piety of the Africans, in contrast to the slovenly and immoral behaviour of the Europeans.

Anna Maria and her husband failed to bring order to the colony and Alexander died, disappointed and drunken, in 1992. His widow quickly married Isaac DuBois and returned home, via Jamaica, where she again had the opportunity to study the slave trade. Her voyage was, she admitted "an unusual enterprize for an Englishwoman."

Harriet Martineau

In the 1830's another strong-minded woman without fear of strange climes was the Bristol-educated writer and social reformer Harriet Martineau, who explored Egypt and investigated the slave trade in America. Respect for womanhood, and deferential colonial attitudes kept these women safer than their modern equivalents might be, and they usually employed guides to fend off beggars and thieves. Exposure to coarse foreign ways and alien religions were not considered a threat to well brought up Victorian ladies.

Travel for the middle classes became widely popular from the mid-19th century, when Thomas Cook pioneered the package tour, sending his first party to Paris in 1855 and the Rhineland the following year. Switzerland and the Alps became a favourite destination for the English, who created an Alpine Club in 1857; Francis Tuckett of Frenchay was one of the founder members.

Although until the mid nineteenth century Australia had been treated as a convenient dumping ground for criminals and other social undesirables by the desperate authorities of England and Ireland, the new land was fast shaking off these undignified associations and emerging as a land of opportunity and new beginnings. Rachel Henning from Bristol set off for Australia in 1854 on the SS Great Britain, and her letters home, describing her new life, became an Australian classic. Rachel (1826-1914) was the eldest daughter of a Bristol clergyman, and when her mother died, she was left responsible for four younger children.

She left with a brother and a sister for Australia, but soon returned, homesick, in 1861. But she made the voyage once more and the second time settled on her brother's Queensland sheep station. She married the overseer and lived on various farms in New South Wales. The delightful and self-revealing letters written to her sisters Amy and Etty, between 1853 and 1882 were never intended for publication, and remained unknown until they were published in 1969.

Amelia Edwards (1831 - 1892)

But the boldest traveller of all was probably Amelia Edwards, who lived in Westbury on Trym, and is buried in Henbury churchyard, under an ankh symbol to denote the great experience of her life: her discovery of ancient Egypt and her great campaign to save its treasures from looters and collectors.

Egyptology was her second career, for at first she earned her living as a writer (another suitable job for a Victorian lady) of - it must be said - fairly trashy novels, full of hectic melodrama. Amelia Edwards, like another jobbing Bristol writer, Emma Marshall, needed to earn a living.

Amelia Edwards was born in London in 1831; her mother was a lively Irishwoman, her father an ex-army officer who worked in a City bank. She was educated at home and early on displayed a talent for music and singing, drawing, and writing. When her father's bank failed, she supported the entire family by writing stories for magazines like Dickens' **Household Words** and **All The Year Round**. She became a staff member of the **Saturday Review** and the **Morning Post**, claiming that as a journalist she eventually covered everything except politics and court reporting. She was certainly versatile; for she wrote poetry, produced summaries of French and English history, and travel books, which she illustrated herself.

Amelia Edwards' illustration of a great rock-cut temple in Nubia

Her first novel, **My Brother's Wife** was published in 1855, when she was only 24. She then turned to sensational stories with foreign settings and lashings of passion and intrigue and titles such as **The 4.15 Express**, and **The Tragedy In Bardello Place**.

All her books are forgotten now but in her day she had great popular success with books such as **Barbara's History**, a novel about bigamy which ran into three editions and was translated into German, Italian and French, and **Lord Brackenbury**, her last novel, about a lord who fakes his own death and then turns himself into an Italian sailor. This one was published with her own illustrations, and was the best seller of them all. Altogether she produced eight novels, two of which drew flattering remarks from Matthew Arnold and Robert Browning.

By the mid 1860s her writing had made her relatively wealthy, and in 1864 she moved to 'The Larches' (demolished by bombing in World War Two) in Eastfield, Westbury on Trym, where she remained for the rest of her life. What drew her to Bristol from London is unknown, but one of her greatest friends was Bristol actor William Mcready.

From this base she travelled extensively with her lifelong friend and companion, Miss Renshawe, always taking notes and sketching. Her first travel book was **Sights and Stories** (1869), an account of a tour of Belgium. She then conceived a passion for mountaineering, and explored the Dolomites, making sketches. Characteristically, she scrambled along muletracks and stayed in primitive lodgings, and lost her luggage over a precipice. On hearing that the Sasso Bianco had never been climbed, she and her companion decided to be the first and after six hours toiling through the mist, they reached the summit and had boiled eggs, bread and brandy. The result of this trip was **Untrodden Peaks And Unfrequented Valleys** (1873).

 She also went to Constantinople, the Levant and Syria, but the visit that was to transform her life at the age of 42, happened by accident. She and Miss Renshawe went on a sketching tour in the south of France but bad weather drove them to find somewhere sunnier, and on a whim they chose to go to Cairo.

As the introduction to her wonderful account of their adventures, **A Thousand Miles Up The Nile** (1877) explains, they did it the hard way. "The choice between dahabeeyah (the flat-bottomed native boat) and steamer is like the choice between travelling with post-horses and travelling by rail. The one is expensive, leisurely, delightful; the other is cheap, swift and comparatively comfortless." Cheap meant in their case £10 a day to cover everything: which must have been an absolute fortune in 1870s Cairo.

How the ladies managed to spend such prodigious amounts soon becomes clear: She set out from Shepherd's Hotel with a boat, a crew of 20 dragomen, plus chickens and sheep and vegetables, and at a leisurely pace she stopped off at every village that interested her, asking where the ancient ruins were, so that she could sketch them, hunt for souvenirs, bones and shards, or scraps of burial robes. Wherever she went she was presented to the local dignitaries and given a feast: the dinner she had with Mustapha Aga, the British Consul, at Luxor in March 1874 was described as "the best meal of our lives that we ate with our fingers. In fact we found them exceedingly useful."

The menu was white soup, fried Samak (a fish), stewed pigeons with spinach and rice, dall, which is roast shoulder of lamb, kebabs of mutton and lamb's kidneys, and tomatoes with rice, turkey with cucumber sauce, pilaff of rice followed by mish mish (preserved apricots), kunafah (rice pudding), Rus Blebban (rice cream) and totleh (sweet jelly).

"Everything was hot, quickly served, admirably dressed, and the best of its kind...Each dipped his own spoon in the soup, dived into

the stew, and pulled pieces of fish or lamb with his fingers. Having no plates, we made plates of our bread. Meanwhile Mustapha Aga, like an attentive host, tore off an especially choice morsel now and then, and handed it to one or other of his guests."

1000 Miles up the Nile is a delightful and dramatic mix of narrative, history, travel and archaeology; Amelia Edwards was a skilled scene setter, a craft learned in writing novels, and her descriptions of people and places are original and witty. She took a wicked delight in satirising the conventional tourists, and a deep interest in the native Egyptians, and she had the endlessly inquiring mind of an academic, so that her accounts of the ruins are meticulous and thorough, though she always wears her scholarship lightly. Often she writes like a poet:

"Then the sun goes down behind the Libyan hills; And the palms stand out black and bronzed against a golden sky; and the Pyramids, left far behind, look grey and ghostly in the distance."

This highly readable work, the first serious attempt in English to describe the antiquities of Egypt, took her an exhausting four years to research, write and illustrate, and it launched her on a new life.

From then on she dropped all other work and devoted her life to rescuing and recording the ancient sites and protecting them, to promoting proper scientific excavation and to policing the illegal trade in antiquities. She became known as "the prophet of Egypt" though she only wrote one more book on the subject, Pharaohs, Fellahs and Explorers, a collection of her lectures, which she delivered on a brilliant tour of America in 1889. She was an energetic speaker with a resonant voice and a clear style, and never made her subject sound dry.

It was this triumphant tour that weakened her health and led to her death. She broke her arm in a fall and insisted on carrying on with her schedule, travelling hundreds of miles to the next engagement. Ill-health combined with grief at the death of Ellen, her companion for the previous 28 years, brought about her own death in 1892. It came after flu, caught on a visit to London Docks to examine antiquities that had arrived for distribution to English and foreign museums.

Little is known of Amelia's private life for she was reticent about it; she was once engaged but broke it off because, she said, the esteem she felt was not enough for marriage. She had one of those passionate and innocent friendships with another woman, and apparently grieved deeply when her much older friend died. She loved her garden at Westbury on

Trym, had an extensive library, and was a firm supporter of the women's suffrage movement, though never one of the "faddists". Her obituarist said that she was sweet-tempered and kept aloof from controversy; as a scholar, "her books are deserving of special praise for the small percentage of errors they contain".

When she died in 1892, she left £5,000 to found a London University Chair in Egyptian Archaeology and Philology, and it is partly thanks to her that Bristol City Museum has some fine exhibits in the Egyptology section.

Since she was not a trained archaeologist or ancient historian, some of her conclusions have since been discounted, but it was she who started serious academic interest in the subject, leading to the foundation in 1882 of the Egyptian Exploration Fund. The fund fuelled popular interest and academic research in a new subject that eventually led Howard Carter and Lord Caernarvon to their famous discoveries in the Valley of the Kings in 1922.

Lady Novelists of the 19th Century

Back home in England, thousands of minor women novelists were scribbling away, sublimating their frustrations and exercising their imaginations, and quite a few of them made a good living out of it. There was an audience of millions of captive women whiling away time at home, needing some easy escapist literature that was also improving, moral and Christian. Bristol was no exception, and although most of the city's writers soon fell into obscurity after brief fame they achieved extraordinary heights of popularity in their day.

Emma Marshall (1830 - 1899)

If there were to be a prize for sheer quantity of output, then Emma Marshall the Victorian novelist would easily win outright. She wrote over 200 novels, short stories, ballads and poems, she wrote for schoolgirl magazines, women's magazines, and Christian journals, and she wrote because she needed the money.

Emma was born in 1830 into an East Anglian banking family of Quakers, who came to live at 2, Victoria Square Clifton. Emma converted to the Church of England and was baptised at Christ Church, Clifton by the Rev. James Marshall, whose banker son Hugh she married. Her mother-in-law wrote improving books of domestic instruction under the pseudonym of Leigh Richmond.

Emma Marshall

The couple set up home in Cotham and then for brief spells in Exeter, and Gloucester and Wells, where despite at that stage having seven children, she began to write under her own name. She had been following in the footsteps of her sister Hannah, and when she died in 1861, Emma completed two of her sister's books. She sent a copy of one of them, ***Emily the Peacemaker***, to the poet Longfellow, and a long postal friendship began. In Clifton Emma became part of the literary circle that included John Addington Symonds.

Then in 1878, when the tally of children was up to nine, Hugh's bank, the West of England, failed. This left the family with huge debts, as they had been major shareholders. The eleven strong Marshall clan constantly moved house, from Weston-super-Mare to Westbury Park to Worcester Terrace, while Emma wrote them out of debt.

Friends helped with the education of the children, but for the remainder of her time Emma had to become a hack writer, taking on every commission that was offered her. She did managed to pull the large family out of trouble and eventually they moved to an impressive house, Ferncliffe in Leigh Woods, but even there, she had to take in boarders from Clifton High School. (When her favourites married, she gave them copies of her work, bound in white leather).

The novels and stories are typical of their time, full of gentle romance and adventure and piety, but she had a lively style and a fertile imagination, and girls of the period obviously found titles such as *Violet Douglas or The Problems of Life*, and *A Lily Among Thorns* an irresistible read. In Bristol she was chiefly famous for her historical novels with a local setting: *In Colston's Days*, *By The Sword Divided*, *Bristol Diamonds* were all big sellers, even if her approach to historical accuracy was a little cloudy, for she depended a great deal on local amateur historians for her facts.

She took to writing novels based on the lives of other writers - *On The Banks of the Ouse* was about poet Cowper, *Under Salisbury Spire* featured George Herbert and *Winchester Meads* Bishop Ken, while *In The East Country* starred Sir Thomas Browne. She also turned to music: In *The Choir of Westminster Abbey* was about Henry Purcell. All these books were politely reviewed in *The Spectator*, *The Athanaeum* or *The Sunday Review*. Some of her books were actually translated into several languages, and one was pirated into French. For the modern reader, they seem a little mimsy in style, but they are certainly still readable and have great period charm, though the factual content often needs to be taken with a pinch of salt.

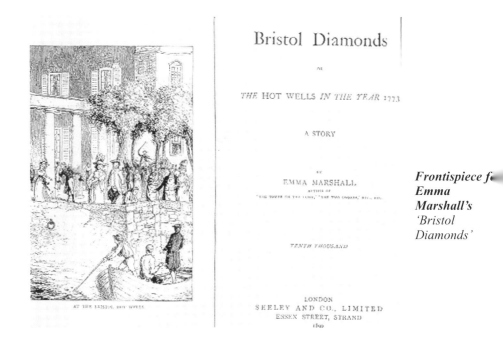

Frontispiece fo Emma Marshall's 'Bristol Diamonds'

In *Bristol Diamonds, A Story of the Hot-wells in 1773*, for example, she has contrived to have her hero and heroine meet Mrs Hannah More at her school at 10, Park Street where by coincidence Edmund Burke has dropped in to take tea (from old Bristol ware) and talk about the American War of Independence and the fate of a consignment of tea due to be shipped from Boston to Bristol. The party all wish him well in the forthcoming election, which shows great prescience, since Burke was not put forward as a parliamentary candidate until October 1774 and the War of Independence began in 1775.

Copies of these Bristol novels often turn up in second-hand bookshops for a few pounds, and one or two people even collect Emma Marshall's work, which as a self-confessed hack writer, would have pleased her. She died in 1899 and is buried in Long Ashton churchyard.

'Michael Field'

Michael Field' was the nom de plume of not one but two women, aunt and niece Edith Emma Cooper (1862-1913) and Katharine Harris Bradley (1864-1914). They were extremely popular in their day, as collaborating dramatists and poets. They were both classical scholars and linguists, and lived together; their friendship was said to be a spiritual one and they pronounced themselves 'closer married' than their friends, the Brownings.

Their works are now totally forgotten but they achieved enormous praise for their play *Calirrhoe*, published in 1884. They chose to write under a man's name because "we have things to say that the world will not tolerate from a woman's lips." They were right; as soon as their identities were revealed, sales dropped and they received little critical attention, so it was just as well that they had a private income.

Altogether the pair wrote 27 dramas, mainly based on history and legend, and a fair number of poems, all pretty unmemorable if this one, on Leonardo's *La Gioconda*, (the Mona Lisa) is anything to go by:

> *Historic, sidelong, implicating eyes;*
> *A smile of velvet's lustre on the cheek;*
> *Calm lips the smile leads upward: hand that lies*
> *Glowing and soft, the patience in its rest*
>
> *Of cruelty that waits and does not seek*
> *For prey; a dusky forehead and a breast*
> *Where twilight touches ripeness amorously;*
> *Behind her, crystal rocks, a sea and skies*
> *Of evanescent blue on cloud and creek;*
> *Landscape that shines suppressive of its zest*
> *For those vicissitudes by which men die.*

E.H. Young (1880 - 1949)

Bust of E.H. Young sculpted by her sister Mrs. Sanderson

One reputation that has been revived dramatically, after decades of neglect, is that of E.H. Young, whose Clifton novels were re-published by Virago Press in the 1980s. Of all the women writers in this book, she had a literary talent that transcended her local interest. She won the Tait Black Memorial Prize for **Miss Mole**, while her novel **William** was selected as one of the first ten books to be published in paperback by Penguin.

Emily Hilda Young was born in Northumberland in 1880, the daughter of a ship-broker. Through a sister she was introduced to Bristol solicitor Arthur Daniell, whom she married in 1902. He came from a cultured legal family who were patrons of the arts - they befriended artist Stanley Spencer and held musical soirees - and sympathetic to the women's suffrage movement, as were E.H.Young and her husband, for they helped put on a feminist play. The Young family were also theatrical, Emily's sister Gladys becoming a well-known actress.

From 1907 the couple lived in Clifton at 2a Saville Place, in the top floor flat. A commemoration plaque marks the spot today. From there, Emily Young cast her cool eye on Clifton society, wandering around in search of settings for her novels, and describing them so accurately that the reader can still recognise the houses and streets she describes, and follow precisely the routes her characters take, across the Downs, down to Queens Road to the shops and back to the handsome villa in Clifton Park.

What she describes, with wit and irony, are the lives and difficult relationships of people who are bound by conventions, and what happens when they ignore them. They make unlikely or unhappy marriages, they nearly cause a scandal by running away, or having liaisons; if they achieve self-knowledge, they do it the hard way.

In *William* (1925) for example, a novel set in Hotwells, on the docks, and up in Clifton, a complacent marriage is rocked by a scandal which the wife refuses to acknowledge. In *Jenny Wren* (1932) and its sequel *The Curate's Wife* (1934) two sisters marry and reap the consequences of choices made for the wrong reasons. *Miss Mole* (1930) is a piercingly accurate account of the diminished and brave existence of a poor spinster living in rooms provided by a mean clergyman employer:

> *Cheerfully she looked about her when she was left alone and she decided she liked this narrow room with its sloping walls, and then with the wariness of an old campaigner, she examined the blankets, which were clean, and the sheets which were rather coarse, and thumped the mattress critically.*

> *"Lumpy" she said, frowning a little. But never mind! She had the view from the window, she thought she would be able to hear the ships hooting up and down the river and not far away there was the real Upper Radstowe with its old streets and crescents, its odd passage and flights of steps, and she unstrapped her box... (Miss Mole)*

The Misses Mallet (1922) shows a wealthy, lazy family of spinster women forced to face reality when a niece goes husband-hunting, and *Celia*, (1937) possibly her finest book, is a deeply complex portrait of a highly attractive woman who sustains her flawed marriage by dreaming of the man she actually wanted, only to find the dream was a piece of harmful self-delusion.

Fleshing out these personal voyages of discovery is a wonderfully comic portrait of Clifton society at all levels, from the shabby boarding houses and the vicarages, to the homes of the old wealth or new money earned in trade, a way of life complete with charity bazaars, outdoor theatre, tramrides, shopping and grand parties, and laced with snobbery and good works and genteel poverty. A surprising extra element is a passionate identification with the countryside that lay the other side of the Suspension Bridge, a magical place where the characters sometimes escape to find their inner selves in a Lawrentian communion with nature:

> *She paid the toll. It was an extravagance when she might have stood for nothing on the little hill overlooking bridge and river, but nowhere else could she get this feeling of being poised, of hovering between earth and water. Though the structure was strong enough, no doubt, it looked as though it had been flung*

across the gulf by a light hand and when she stood on it, between the tall railings at the edge and the curved girder on the other side of the footpath, she liked to believe that a strong gust of wind might catch her up and fling her beyond these barriers, and to know meanwhile that she was safe.. (Celia)

In all there are eight Clifton novels, the last of them being ***Chatterton Square*** (1947) which is set in Canynge Square, and is a merciless dissection of a hypocritical husband and father.

E. H. Young was writing about Clifton (which she called Upper Radstowe) long after she left it, as if every nook and cranny was engraved on her mind: her affection for it shines through every novel and all the major characters, at some point, give thanks "for living in this place and no other."

Emily stayed in Bristol throughout the First World War, but left the city immediately afterwards. Her husband tried to enlist in 1914 but at forty was rejected as being too old. As trench warfare thinned out hundreds of thousands of young men he was finally called up in 1916, and was killed at Ypres in 1917. What effect his death had on Emily we have no record; only that she worked in a local munitions factory in Bristol, and also as a groom in a local stables. Immediately after the war she left Bristol for London, never to live in Clifton again.

Emily was a pioneer of women's climbing, recording in one of her few autobiographical pieces of writing how as late as 1913 "a woman in knickerbockers was an object of derision or shame... the skirt was decently worn for as long as possible, then hidden under a rock" for retrieval on the way down. Since 1906 she had been taking climbing holidays in Wales with - among others - Ralph Bushell Henderson, who like Daniell had been educated at Bristol Grammar School. After the war she left her beloved Clifton to live in a mènage-à-trois with Henderson, who was soon to become Headmaster of Alleyn's School, Dulwich, and his wife Beatrice. Henderson had contracted a shotgun marriage at the age of twenty-one, when Beatrice was six months pregnant. Had he divorced, he would have lost his job. For more than twenty years, until his retirement in 1940, the three of them preserved a façade of respectability.

Emily then bought a house in Bradford-on-Avon, presumably with the proceeds from her books. Henderson lived with her there, outfacing small-town gossip, while Mrs Henderson went to live in Weston-super-Mare, where she died in 1961. Emily, a heavy smoker, died of lung cancer in 1949. "Life without Emily is just one long, long pain" Henderson wrote to his sister.

Emily left no letters or diaries to give a clue to her feelings. As a climber she was said to display remarkable qualities of balance, speed, leadership and sound judgemnent - qualities which surely enabled her to live a fulfilled, balanced and unconventional life.

Barbara Pym (1913 - 1980)

Barbara Pym lived in Bristol for part of the Second World War. She had grown up in Oswestry, Shropshire, and after three happy years at Oxford taking a degree in English Literature had returned there, writing novels which failed to find a publisher in between the light domestic duties of a daughter at home. In April 1940 her younger sister Hilary, who worked for the BBC, had been evacuated with them to Bristol, and Barbara began to envy her independent life. In 1941 matters were taken out of her hand when she was 'called up' and, thanks to her German, got a job with the Censorship Department (German division), housed in the Royal West of England Academy.

Barbara joined Hilary at The Coppice, a large house in Leigh Woods, from where they would cross the Suspension Bridge every day to go to work. The Coppice was home to a small community of women and children who appear to have had great fun, despite (or because of) wartime conditions. It was an unhappy love affair with a married man that decided Barbara to leave Bristol after two years. She joined the WRENS in July 1943 and was posted to Italy.

After the war Barbara and Hilary shared a series of homes in London. During the 1950s Barbara published six novels, including *No Tame Gazelle* and *A Glass of Blessings*. She gained a steady following for her wry stories of women's lives told in a distinctive, ironical voice. When her seventh novel was rejected by her publisher in the early

1960s, because it did not reflect the youthful culture of the time, it was a dreadful shock to her. She went on writing novels for a further fourteen years, though with no hope of publishing them. Then, in January 1977, her life was transformed, when both Philip Larkin and Lord David Cecil named her as the most under-rated writer of the century in a *Times Literary Supplement* article. Suddenly her books were in demand again. Her novel *Quartet in Autumn*, about four single people in an office on the verge of retirement, was short-listed for the Booker Prize. Review comments like 'This quietly powerful novel' and 'An exquisite, even magnificent, work of art' made up for all the years of frustration and disappointment.

Barbara Pym did not have long to enjoy her fame - which included having a TV programme made about her called 'Tea with Miss Pym'. She died of cancer of the stomach in January 1980. Today there is a flourishing Barbara Pym Society based at her old Oxford college, St Hilda's.

Mary Renault (1905 - 1983)

Eileen Mary Challens, whose pen name was Mary Renault, was a pupil at Clifton High School. Her father was a doctor who came to Bristol from London, and from an early age his daughter declared her desire to be a writer. From Clifton, Eileen went to St. Hugh's college, Oxford, to read English, from where she graduated in 1928. In 1937 she qualified as a state registered nurse, and a year later, had her first novel accepted. Several others followed, but despite high literary earnings she continued to work as a nurse during World War two, until she won the MGM prize, which gave her financial independence.

Her early novels had contemporary settings, and often dealt with homo-sexual or bisexual relationships. She took up this theme in her most famous series of historical novels set in Ancient Greece and Asia. There were eight of these novels, the best-sellers being The Bull from the sea, The King must Die, The Persian Boy and the Mask of Apollo. Most of them are still in print. Mary Renault's novels are notable for their careful research, poetic style and sympathetic portrayal of homosexual love. These novels of her mature years were written after she had emigrated to South Africa with her partner, Julie Mullard, where they were opponents of the Apartheid regime.

Deborah Moggach

Clifton with its special flavour and identity, has always inspired writers: two of them, both students at Bristol University in the Sixties, set their first novels there. One was Deborah Moggach, who set her novel in a seedy flat, probably in Freeland Place:

> *It was one of the humble crescents that crowd round the hill, at the top of which stood grandest Clifton with the tall balconied houses, at the bottom of which stood the less grand Clifton with its rivers, warehouses and shabby pubs.*
> *The front doors of Jacob's Crescent led straight out onto the pavement; number 18 was shamefully run down. Its owner lived elsewhere and had done nothing to it. The ground floor was empty with boards across the windows. Upstairs on the first floor was also empty. She put down the shopping and went to the window. The city was spread before her, its spires, its docks, its glittering office buildings, and faint on the horizon, its suburbs. Down below she could see the strips of garden that belonged to her neighbours; number 18's was full of junk tangled up among the thistles.*
> *(You Must Be Sisters 1978)*

The other was *Angela Carter* (1940 - 1991), whose first novel, originally called Shadow Dance, is located in the student-land of Clifton at a time when even the grand terraces were run-down and dilapidated, Angela Carter describes the old Regent Street auction rooms (now redeveloped as flats and a pizza restaurant) which once that had been part of the Cordeux department store:

> *The auction sales were held in the gutted corpse of what had once been an Edwardian department store, where tall thin pillars topped with fading garlands of gilded leaves insinuated hints of departed elegancies among the heaped junk around them, and strangely placed long mirrors, flyblown, in dark corners, suddenly aston-ished you with your own speckled reflection. It was quiet, dark and soothing. Morris sucked up eagerly the smell of dirt, poverty and graveclothes... the best times in his life were the dark nights when, in Honeybuzzard's van, they went secretly to the deserted,*

condemned old houses which the city council planned shortly to demolish and, by the light of guttering candles, would sort over and pick about in all their dead flotsam.
(Honeybuzzard 1966).

Poets

Helen Dunmore

As far as we can tell, Bristol has produced no major women poets until this century. Ursula Fanthorpe who was born 1929, educated at Oxford and taught at Cheltenham Ladies College, became a middle-aged drop-out to set herself free to write. She worked as a hospital records clerk at Burden Neurological Institute, where her first poems, about the hospital and patients, were written and published. She won the Arvon prize in 1980 and has since published several collections of poems.

Helen Dunmore is the latest Bristol poet and novelist to win prizes in both fields, and considerable critical acclaim. In 1996 she won the Orange Prize for Fiction, a controversial award which is open to women writers only.

Women Artists

It is still insufficiently recognised today how many women artists there were in the nineteenth century, and how influential they were, even though they were often admired by their contemporaries.

Rolinda Sharples (1793-1838)

Bristol's Rolinda Sharples seems to have been accepted as a professional, for she was allowed, rather like a modern press photographer, to be present to sketch at major Bristol events, such as the trial of Colonel Brereton, after the Bristol Riots of 1831. This remains perhaps her most famous portrait, with 46 figures, all of whom are identifiable as portraits of those present at the court martial in the great Room of the Merchants Hall. Naughtily, she includes a portrait of herself making the sketch for the painting.

Rolinda's mother Ellen was also a respected local patron of the arts, and it was she who helped found, with the gift of £2,000, the Fine Arts Academy that was to become the modern Royal West of England Academy. On her death in 1948 she left the institution £3,465 and some paintings. This at least was an institution open to women; when classes were started in 1845, a special women-only life class was arranged.

The entire Sharples family were artists: James, a portrait painter from Bath, his wife Ellen, a miniaturist, son James and daughter Rolinda all painted for a living and made a good one. The husband and wife were especially successful in America, where they worked from 1784 to 1802; they had commissions to paint portraits of leading political figures such as Washington and Jefferson.

Clifton Race Course, 1836, *Rolinda Sharples.*

In 1802 the family returned home for a few years, but fears of invasion by Napoleon sent them back in 1806, to New York, where James died in 1811. Ellen Sharples and her children came back to Bristol and settled first at the Sion Bath House (next door to St. Vincent Rocks Hotel) and finally at 3, St. Vincent's Parade, Hotwells, where in the 1780's James Sharples had worked as a portraitist at the Hotwell spa.

Mrs. Sharples kept a diary in which she noted her daughter's educational and artistic progress. "Drawing, reading and instructing my dear Rolinda continues greatly to interest me... I delight to instruct her in arithmetic, natural philosophy, I attend to her reading, drawing, geography and French." She would encourage visual observation by taking Rolinda to observe famous Bristol sights, like the rowdy St. James Fair, or the races on the Downs. She also took her children to concerts, the theatre, and museums, and drew up for them an impressive reading list. Under her mother's guidance Rolinda went to London especially to view the Elgin Marbles, and to see the actor Kean playing Iago in Othello.

At 13, "Rolinda drew the portrait of a young lady of her acquaintance in crayons, which was greatly admired... and which decided her becoming a professional artist. The praises bestowed on her performances, with the small gold pieces in exchange, were very exhilarating and made her apply with delighted interest, improving rapidly," her mother noted. Ellen was deliberately equipping her daughter to become financially independent, should she not marry, as turned out to be the case.

> *Rolinda would have resources within herself should a diminution or loss of fortune ever be experienced. I have frequently thought that every well-educated female, particularly those who have only small fortunes, should at least have the power, if they did not exercise it, by the cultivation of some available talent, of obtaining the conveniences and some of the elegances of life.*

So Rolinda was given a studio where she set up a portrait practice in fashionable Clifton; she exhibited at the Royal Academy for the first time in 1820, when of the 540 artists on show, 41 were women. She also exhibited in Carlisle, Liverpool, Leeds and Dublin, and in 1827 became an honorary member of the Royal Society of British Artists, a sign that she was thoroughly accepted by the establishment..

Her most famous paintings are panoramic chronicles of Bristol life: she painted St. James Fair, the Bristol Races, the Rownham Ferry, the Market; if necessary she would hire a room overlooking the scene she was painting. She liked to paint scenes where local people were identifiable, such as the ***Cloakroom At Clifton Assembly*** (now the Clifton Club and a room looking much the same as it does in the painting).

Rolinda kept a diary, most of which is now sadly lost. There is a record of her observing the 1830 visit to the Clifton Hotel and Assembly Rooms by the Duchess of Kent and her daughter Princess Victoria, who was 11 at the time: "...spent the day Duchess hunting.... the best view that we had of the Duchess and the Princess was from the window of the hotel at which they stood a long time repeatedly curtseying." She also painted another major event in Bristol, *The Stoppage Of The Bank*. These set pieces survive but very few of the hundreds of portraits she did have surfaced, in Bristol at least, thought the City Art Gallery has a fair number of her works. She was not a great artists but she was certainly a competent one, who left a useful social record of her time.

Sadly Rolinda died from cancer at the age of 44, at the height of her powers, leaving us to only guess at how her work might have developed. No other woman painter from Bristol achieved such fame in her own city, but another did achieve it - in Paris.

Paule Vezelay (1892-1984)

'In a restaurant', an oil painting by Paule Vezelay

Paule Vezelay was so keen to shed her Bristol life that she invented her name: she was born Margery Watson-Williams, daughter of a Clifton ear nose and throat specialist; she was educated at Clifton High School and spent three years at the Art school in Bristol before leaving for London and the Slade.

139

There she was put in a beginners class where the teaching seemed to her so elementary and academic that she walked out after four or five sessions, and enrolled in the London School of Art in South Kensington. There the students drew from life, using models from the street, and she also went to lithography classes at the Chelsea Polytechnic. Though classes stopped with the outbreak of World War One, Vezelay was able to get work and her first success was the illustrating of *A Diary Of The Great War* by Samuel Pepys junior, an anonymous parody, with black and white illustrations in the style of Beardsley. In 1917 she won a commission to illustrate five articles on aspect s of London life, for the periodical *Drawing and Design*. She was subsequently asked to illustrate another book, and it looked as this stage as she would gain recognition as a lithographer and etcher, not as a painter.

But a visit to Paris in 1920 changed her life, and her name. She found in Paris the art that stimulated her imagination and from then on she spent a large part of her working life in Paris, developing a style that was bold and simple, with high key colours and a strong design content.

At her first show in London in 1921, she exhibited some vividly formalised scenes of circus life, of restaurants and theatres and she soon became known as one of the earliest British abstract painters. She became a member of the London Group in 1922 and organised for a big exhibition in 1925, where her work was shown in the company of contributions from Nash, Epstein, and Nicholson.

In 1926 she decided to settle in Paris for good and adopt a new persona. Her style needed a European- sounding name to go with it, one which cut her free from Bristol and London, so she chose Paule Vezelay and was known by that name for the rest of her life - it was if she had reinvented herself. During this period she met Picasso, Bracque, Kandinsky, Arp and Gris, and her work began to show the influence of Cubism. She joined the group Abstract-Creation in 1934, and exhibited regularly in Paris, until war drove her back home to Bristol to look after her parents, just at a time when her work was fruitful and well-recognised.

She remained in Bristol through the Blitz, and spent three years in the city caring for her parents. She lived in Henleaze and then Clifton, seldom able to work, and feeling totally isolated as an artist, until she won permission to make some drawings of the bombed city. (Censorship rules prevented artists sketching where they pleased, in case they handed over useful information to the enemy).

Vezelay had been turned down as an official war artist but she went to see Sir Kenneth Clark, then the chairman of the War Artists Advisory Committee, who sanctioned her sketching in Bristol and bought one of her drawings, which is now in the City Art Gallery. In 1942 she found solace in making studies of the barrage balloon centre (run by the women's services, incidentally) just outside Bristol. The strange abstract beauty of the shapes appealed to her, and she saw the series of drawings as her contribution to the war effort.

In 1942 she moved to London and showed her balloon drawings and some abstract paintings at an exhibition that year. She sat the rest of the war out in London, intending to go straight back to Paris once peace had been declared, but once there she found that the atmosphere had changed and the art scene she knew had vanished. She returned to London for good, living irascibly at Barnes, and always missing Paris. Paule did some textile designs for Heals in the 1940s, and in 1949 was made a member of the Society of Industrial Artists and Designers.

After a fallow period of ten years, she began to paint again and was given a show in the Grosvenor Galleries in London and in Zabriskie's in New York. Her work never became particularly famous, but it was respected enough for her to have a major exhibition at the Tate Gallery in 1983, where she showed her thread collages, lines of cord suspended in patterns under glass, her wood reliefs, and some of her cool classical abstracts which had a very Fifties minimalism about them.

In a television interview with Germaine Greer, a few months before her death, she said: "English Art bored me to tears... the English don't like originality in Art very much you know." She died in 1984, one of the few British artists whose devotion to the abstract movement never faltered.

Dorothy Woollard (1886-1986)

Bristol produced no other women artists of great note, but Dorothy Woollard at least won a distinguished reputation as an etcher and printmaker. The publishers A.C. Black chose her as artist for some of their famous Sketch Book series, and she was the natural choice for the Bristol volume, produced in 1926.

She studied and then taught at the Bristol Municipal School of Art, as a pupil of Reginald Bush, whom she nursed in his old age. In 1914 Woollard won a scholarship to the Royal College of Art in London and her studies too were interrupted by World War One, which she spent drawing maps for the Admiralty. She moved permanently to London in 1922, and lived on a pittance, grateful for any commission from her home city such as the book plate for the Bristol Museum and Art Gallery brochure. She also did a series of prints of Bristol scenes for the Bristol art firm Frost and Reed.

Temple Back c. 1915, Dorothy Woollard

As an artist in the etching medium, she had a painterly approach, reviving the art of stipple engraving and intaglio, which gave her landscapes and portraits a depth and luminosity, and there is evident humour in her approach to the street scenes. But the medium was limited and she found it hard to make a living. In the second World War she worked as a censor and then when she was in her sixties, she started translating medical books into Braille, and for the latter half of her life - she lived to be 100 - hardly worked as an artist at all.

The cover of 'A Sketch Book' by Dorothy Woollard

Gwendoline Cross (1900 - 1966)

Woollard was one of a group of women etchers who flourished in Bristol before World War Two during the period when there was a major revival of etching and print-making skills; another was Gwendoline Cross who against her parents' wishes enrolled at the School of Art in 1921, and became a part-time teacher there until 1944. In the mid-Thirties she was one of the founding members of the New Bristol Art Club, which aimed to wake up the city art scene. Her etchings of Bristol scenes are full of atmosphere. She was a versatile artist, painting portraits and still lifes, and working in silver and enamel, as well as finding work as a book illustrator.

Also from the same school are Hilda Hutchings and Kathleen Jebb who both taught at the Municipal School of Art, and exhibited regularly at the Royal West of England Academy, and Olive Stephens, who went to Redland High School and then the School of Art, and who exhibited at the Royal Academy and in Chicago and Los Angeles. Several of these women etchers provided minute prints to go in the cabinets in the library of Queen Mary's Dolls' House at Windsor Castle.

Clifton from the Avon, 1928, Gwendoline Cross

6   Unionists and Suffragettes

Members of the National Federation of Women Workerson the eve of the First World War. The Federation grew out of the National Union of Working Women, founded in Bristol in 1874

In 1868 a number of women, together with a few men, converged on the home of Matthew Davenport Hill at 3 West Mall, Clifton. They were responding to the invitation sent out by Francis Newman, which stated that "Commissioner Davenport Hill permits his daughter, Miss Florence Davenport, to issue it." This meeting was to give birth to the Suffrage Movement in Bristol two years after the inauguration of the movement in London.

Many of those who were active in the suffrage movement had connections with other reform movements, such as the Anti Corn Law League, in London and the Midlands. Families involved in political reform also married into each other. Most of the Bristol supporters would have known each other and many would have worked together in the Anti-Slavery Society.

144

At the meeting in West Mall was Mary Estlin, the Unitarian daughter of a physician who had attended Lant Carpenter's family. She became Treasurer to what was soon to become the **Bristol and West of England Society for Women's Suffrage**. It is probable that Mary Carpenter herself did not attend, although she became a sponsor of the Society, as did Eliza Walker Dunbar. For tactical reasons - not wishing to give the authorities further reason to hamper her work with Bristol's street children - Mary was not an active supporter, although shortly before her death she consented to speak at a large suffrage rally in Bristol. But her work in the reformatories and 'ragged schools' had inspired many women, who became active members. Rosamund and Florence Davenport, and Agnes Beddoe, a doctor's wife, had all assisted Mary Carpenter in her work and she may have been instrumental in introducing the Winkworth sisters to Clifton society when they moved from Manchester in 1864.

Others who were active from the first were the three Quaker sisters, Margaret Tanner and Anna Maria and Mary Priestman. The Priestman sisters were radical liberals, already experienced in the agitation against the Corn Laws and in the Anti-Slavery campaign. They were related to active social campaigners Lilias Ashworth Hallett and Helen Bright Clark, and, together with Emily Sturge, they all became leading speakers in the movement.

The Growing Movement

During the next few years meetings were held in public halls, attracting working women as well as the largely middle-class activists: the areas covered included Bristol, the West Country and North and South Wales. By 1871 early speaking tours were organised, addressed by speakers such as Millicent Fawcett (sister of Elizabeth Garrett Anderson) who led the Suffrage Movement from 1867 onwards, and two other sisters from this militant family, Rhoda and Agnes Garrett. It must have taken a great deal of courage to address large meetings and to undertake speaking tours. Lilias Ashworth Hallett became an experienced speaker nationally as well as in the West Country, but she wrote "The tours of meetings, consisting of six or seven in a fortnight were a great nervous effort in those early days." The meetings were packed by those curious to see and hear these women and were surprised to find quietly dressed ladies who spoke "in a most clear, lucid and persuasive manner."

The Suffrage movement reached a peak of activity in 1880 when the Colston Hall was packed out with 3000 women who had turned up to hear speakers including Emily Sturge and Agnes Beddoe, and an overflow meeting had to be arranged. Soon after this, differences emerged as to the extent of women's aims and the best tactics to be used. Nationally, these differences were shown by the separation of the Women's Social and Political Union (WSPU) from the National Union of Women's Suffrage Societies led by Millicent Fawcett. Emmeline and Christabel Pankhurst led the WSPU and adopted increasingly militant tactics.

Lilias Ashworth Hallett

Industrial Unrest

Intense activity continued throughout the 1870s and 1880s, especially in the period leading up to the Third Reform Bill which gave the vote to County ratepayers in 1884, although still excluded all women. The Priestman sisters had felt so strongly about "taxation without representation" that they had refused to pay their rates, with the result that the bailiffs were sent in and seized their dining-room chairs and other objects to sell at auction. Anna Maria Priestman, together with Emily Sturge and Helen Bright Clark, saw their struggle as part of a wider one for democracy and rights for women in employment. In 1875 Anna Maria spoke at the British Association Meeting in Bristol on 'The Industrial Position of Women as Affected by their Exclusion from the Suffrage', arguing that women needed union organisation as well as the vote. She was active in supporting the strike of the cotton workers of Barton Hill in 1889 although not a member of the Bristol Socialist Society.

Helena Born and Miriam Daniell

Bristol by 1889 was seething with industrial discontent, with spontaneous strikes initiated in an unco-ordinated fashion by mainly unskilled men and women, especially among the dockers, railway workers and in the cotton and chocolate industries. Prominent among the Bristol Socialists who helped to organise the strikers were Helena Born and Miriam Daniell. Helena had left Clifton to live in the working class area of St Philips, declaring "I feel that the only effectual way to convince others of the truth of ones (Socialist) principles, and to bring about the new time, is to live them". Miriam had also left her husband to live with Helena. Public hostility to this Socialist, Lesbian relationship was stoked and the women eventually left England for a utopian socialist community in America. But while in Bristol they took a leading role in establishing a Strike Organisation Committee to support the women cotton workers of the Barton Hill factory, and, in 1889, the Sander's Confectionery Workers, where women and girl workers were resisting the firm's attempts to enforce an intensification of work, while refusing to allow them to form a trade union.

Barton Hill Cotton workers

The strike lasted a terrible 23 weeks and ended in the failure of their objectives, but the trend for Bristol working women to become militantly organised was established, and arguably had a more conciliatory effect on the employer and worker relations in the forthcoming decades. The Quaker Fry's chocolate factory, for example, introduced welfare benefits for its largely female workforce after being hit by industrial action in the same year, and other Bristol firms such as Wills Tobacco and Mardons the printers followed suit.

Enid Stacey became secretary of the Sander's strike committee, and was the first recipient of a Catherine Winkworth scholarship to Bristol University. She was victimised for her socialist activities by Redland High School, where she had been a student and subsequently a tutor. She left Bristol to work for the Independent Labour Party, and died at the age of 35 in 1903. Sylvia Pankhurst wrote that she had "undermined her originally fine physique by unresting labours, constant open-air speaking, constant journeying, poor food, and uncomfortable quarters."

Emma Smith (1852 - 1886)

The first Trades Union for women workers was founded by Emma Smith. She was the daughter of a schoolmaster, and had come to Bristol on her marriage to Thomas Paterson, a self-educated philosopher and secretary of working mens' clubs in the city.

Emma read a paper on the plight of working women to the Social Science Congress in Bristol, and followed this up with a meeting to set up a union for women. To avoid alarming Bristol's middle-class susceptibilities, it was not called a union, but the more comfortingly gallant Women's Protective and Provident League. The dangerous 'U' word was not used publically until the founding in Bristol of the first-ever trade union for women, the National Union of working Women, in 1874.

The organisation flourished, and Emma found an ally in Edith Simcox, an intellectual who ran a workroom for Bristol shirtmakers - one of the customers was Edith's novelist friend, George Eliot, who had all her underwear made there. Networking is not a new idea.
Emma and Edith startled employers and industrialists by turning up at the previously all-male Trades Union Congress in 1875, demanding equal pay for women. Edith spelled it out: "Hitherto the rate of women's wages has ended where that of men began. I would have women refuse to do men's work for less than men's wages." It was to take another hundred years before parity was achieved.

Emma Paterson improved the lot of Bristol women in other ways, by starting clubs for working women, rest and reading rooms, and a popular swimming club. She also edited a journal, wrote articles, addressed meetings, lectured at universities, and campaigned ceaselessly for improvement to women's working conditions, insisting that the struggle should be continued collectively, through trades unions.

Emma ended up poorer than the women she fought for, limiting herself to an expenditure of sixpence a day, and driving herself so mercilessly that she died aged only 34. She was instrumental in starting 30 unions covering as many women's trades, and is honoured at Congress House in London.

The Journey Towards the Vote

Thanks to the Municipal Franchise act of 1869, women householders were allowed to vote. In Bristol this meant that 2,465 women could vote for the first time in local elections. In some areas, this actually amounted to political clout: in Clifton, for example, where there were 1,907 male burgesses or rate payers, there were now 641 women entitled to vote and influence the result. By 1880 there were 830 eligible Clifton women ratepayers.

Women were not eligible to stand for local elections until 1907. Several large boroughs and councils throughout Britain elected women councillors but reactionary Bristol hung back. Helen Sturge stood twice in the local elections, but was considered to be a militant by the voters, and was rejected. Her sister Elizabeth recalled:

> *On one of these occasions as she was returning home after the official counting of the votes, during which she had watched her opponent's pile grow higher and higher, in contrast to her own poor little heap, she heard a man call out from the house she was passing, 'Has the Suffragette got in?' 'I am the Suffragette', she politely informed him, as she went on her way.*

The Bristol Suffragettes

Annie Kenney

Women carried on the struggle for fairer working conditions and universal female suffrage into the early twentieth century. Associated with Christabel Pankhurst was Annie Kenney, a Lancashire mill-girl, who worked full-time for WSPU and was sent to Bristol as organiser of the Suffragettes in the West of England from 1907 - 1909. Christabel and Annie had been the first suffragettes to suffer a prison sentence in 1908. In Annie, Christabel found a devoted follower, and one who was able to inspire devotion in others. Among her ardent supporters was Mary Blathwayt, daughter of Colonel and Mrs Blathwayt of Eagle House, Batheaston. Mary spent much of her time in Bristol and travelled with Annie on speaking tours, while her parents provided rest and care at their home for Annie and other workers, worn-out by their work or ill after imprisonment and the barbarism of forced-feeding.

In November 1907 a large meeting was held in the Victoria Rooms at which Mrs Pethick Lawrence and Christabel Pankhurst spoke and a bouncer was employed to eject heckling students. The following year there was a mass rally on the Downs attracting a crowd of 10,000. Rowdy youths tried to disrupt the meeting by ringing bells and shouting "Go home and do the washing!"

Theresa Garnett

In 1909 Theresa Garnett, who lived at 5 York Place, attacked Winston Churchill with a dog-whip at Temple Meads Station because he opposed votes for women, saying "Take that for the women of England!" She was imprisoned in Holloway where she joined two other Clifton women, Mrs Dove Willcox and May Allen. All three went on hunger strike and were forcibly fed. After their release they were afforded a "right royal reception"; a procession met them at Temple Meads with a military band and carriages decorated in the white, green and purple colours of the movement. That year Clifton got its first woman councillor, Emily Harriet Smith.

In May 1909 two activists, Vera Wentworth and Elsie Howey, memorably disrupted a meeting at the Colston Hall, Bristol. Annie Kenney gave the following account of it:

Mr Birrell (Cabinet Minister) was to address a great meeting. We decided to hide in the famous organ. There was a concert the night previous. Two Suffragettes not known in Bristol attended the concert and when it was over went to the ladies' cloakroom and hid themselves. The watchman came on his round but discovered no-

one. Then the Suffragettes did their rounds with the aid of a flash lamp. The only suitable hiding-place near the platform they could find was inside the organ! They discovered a splendid seat on some scaffolding, and so they prepared. They slept by turns during the night and when dawn came they breakfasted on a bar of chocolate, an apple and a roll. Morning arrived, and with it the charwomen all joking about the Suffragettes. They searched every crevice, except of course the one where the Suffragettes were hidden. Then there was a real search by men in the afternoon, and they heard the sigh of relief, "No Suffragettes". The great hall soon filled. The organ started, the noise, the wind, and the vibration nearly knocked the Suffragettes off their high perch. Louder the organ pealed; greater became the excitement of the two extra human pipes attached to it. The vast audience cheered as leading politicians came on the platform.

At last the Minister started his oration. He was getting on famously and was in the middle of one of his most telling sentences when suddenly there resounded through the hall a shrill voice "Votes for Women! Give Women their political freedom!" You can picture the consternation! Where in the world were those women? The audience looked to the ceiling as though they thought anything was possible. Stewards scampered here, there and everywhere. The Suffragettes from their hiding-place watched and enjoyed the scene through chinks in the organ. Things settled down. No Suffragette could be found anywhere and the Minister resumed. He was labouring a point about "Liberty". "Why don't you give the women liberty, then?" suddenly came the same shrill voice. Then there was a scuffle. The audience was convulsed at the predicament of the stewards. The Suffragettes were in the organ. But how could they reach them? The hall was in a uproar. Everybody suggested ways and means to everybody else. They got a ladder, but by the time they got the ladder to one place the Suffragettes had scrambled to the other side, making speeches all the time. After long and strenuous efforts they were captured and cast into the street. The night and day spent in the organ had, however, served its purpose." Incredible though it seems, the Suffragettes succeeded in repeating the performance in the same place!

The successful tactic of interrupting meetings continued. The Bishop of Bristol chaired a meeting in 1914 when a woman rose up to denounce the torture of women in English prisons. A similar denunciation was made before a large audience at a cinema. The Suffrage movement continued to organise meetings and combined with WSPU in many non-violent activities. It was a Suffragist who dropped a petition into the King's carriage when he visited Bristol on July 4th 1913. **'The Suffragette'** reported that 'one of the equerries riding beside the King's carriage deliberately raised his sword and dealt the woman a hard blow'. She was, however, released from Bridewell Police Station without charge at the King's request.

Park Street through a haze of smoke from the burning Suffragettes' Headquarters

In 1913 and 1914 more violent tactics were adopted by the Suffragettes. Fires were started in various parts of the country in November 1913, apparently precipitated by the arrest and sentencing of a well-known Suffragette. A beautiful old house at Frenchay, Begbrook, was gutted and on a pedestal in front of the house was a copy of *'The Suffragette'* with written on it, "Birrell is coming. Rachel Peace is still being tortured".

On October 23rd 1913 a group of militant suffragettes burned down the University's sports pavilion at Coombe Dingle. Retribution was swift. On October 24th at 5pm, 400 or 500 students rushed over to the Suffragette's headquarters opposite the Museum, smashed the plate glass window and threw out the contents to be burned. The upper floor was then wrecked, furniture and papers thrown out and a huge bonfire lit in the middle of the road, around which the students sang and danced. A fascinated crowd gathered until the police sent for fire engines to extinguish the flames, and cleared the road for traffic once more.

Not all members of the WSPU approved of the destruction of buildings and property and Mary Blathwayt resigned, a step that must have been taken with great reluctance and pain. But when World War 1 started on August 4th 1914, the Suffragette response was swift and surely judged. The WSPU discontinued all militant activity, and *The Suffragette* stopped publication. Many of the women threw themselves into war work and distinguished themselves. Theresa Garnett nursed at the front, and was decorated by her old enemy, Winston Churchill. Even before the war was over, a Women's Suffrage Bill was introduced in 1917 and finally passed in February 1918. Women were given the vote but not before the age of 30, and only if they were married, or owned property, or held a degree. It took another ten years for women to obtain equal rights with men.

Female munitions workers at the Bristol Strachan and Henshaw Factory 1915

Lady Apsley and Jennie Lee

Once the votes for women battle had been won, after the First World War, Bristol stopped being a hotbed of feminism. The women who took on men's work were sacked and "went home to do the washing". It says a great deal about the city that it took until the 1943 to accept a woman MP.

In 1942 Lord Apsley, Conservative MP for central Bristol, died on active service. His wife had been caretaking the seat in his absence until then and was politically very active, despite a hunting accident that left her confined to a wheelchair. She became the Conservative candidate at the by-election, standing against the Labour candidate, Jennie Lee. Campaigning on a platform of national unity, Lady Apsley won the seat handsomely for the coalition government. Ten top Tories came to the city to speak on her behalf, and she polled 5,687 votes against Jennie Lee's 4,308.

Jennie Lee made the ***Beveridge Report*** the platform for her campaign. This report was to become the basis of the future welfare state. She attracted plenty of publicity with her travelling barrel organ and nightly public meetings, attended by current and future luminaries such as Stafford Cripps, Mervyn Stockwood, Tom Driberg and the young Michael Foot. She treated the by-election result as a personal disaster, for she had thought it a highly winnable seat and had fought it with all her showbiz inspiration. The problem was that she stood without the approval of the International Labour Party, who accused her of carpet-bagging and fielded their own candidate against her, ruinously splitting the vote.

In the landslide labour election of 1945, Jennie won the seat of Cannock, a mining town in Leicestershire. She held the seat until 1970, when she was defeated and went into the House of Lords. She was made the first Minister for Arts when Harold Wilson put her in charge of establishing the Arts Council in 1964, and, subsequently, the Open University.

In post-war Bristol women gradually began to join in the running of the city and many more became city councillors, magistrates and senior administrators, and legislation on Equal Opportunity and Equal Pay, with a general acceptance that most women wanted to work, eventually changed the previously male culture of the city.

The first woman Lord Mayor in Bristol was Alderman Florence Brown, a trade unionist, who was voted to the office in 1963, though it took until the 1990s before the city council appointed any female chief executives. In the year 2000, three Bristol MP's are women and Bristol Cathedral now has an honorary canon, the Rev. Chairman Mann, and a book of this kind is probably no longer necessary.

And it is worth pointing out that dozens of pioneering women mentioned in this record of lost voices, only a tiny minority of them ever married or had children. Women such as Hannah More, Mary Carpenter and Elizabeth Blackwell, achieved all they did by single-minded dedication. If they had married, running a home and bringing up a family would have taken up the time and energy they devoted to their cause. As Virginia Woolf famously observed: "A woman must have money and a room of her own."

It is only the artists, entertainers and writers who managed to combine marriage, motherhood and work, usually because their partners were from the same world, and sympathised with the creative urge, or simply appreciated the earning power of their wives.

But in the middle of the 20th century, it would have been very hard for a financially dependent wife to work in any field of which her husband disapproved, and those who opted to remain single and independent of constraints, in order to follow their vocations, found that working alone was a hard road to follow and turned to their own sex for support. These women believed in sisterhood, and quite a few of them had women partners; some of these were clearly lesbian relationships, at a time when the subject was barely discussed.

It is hard from a 21st century perspective, to appreciate how brave and original and adventurous these pioneering women were, working as they did against the social grain, confounding the usual expectations about what women could and should do.

Bristol's three women MP's.in 2000. From left to right, Valerie Davey, Dawn Primarolo and Jean Corston.

Bibliography

Catriona Blake, *Eliza Walker Dunbar, The Change of the Parasols: Women's Entry to the Medical Profession*, The Women's Press Ltd., 1990

Bristol Broadsides, *Bristol's Other History*, Bristol Broadside Co-op Ltd., 1983

S Bryher, *A History of the Labour and Socialist Movement in Bristol*

Don Carelton, *A University for Bristol*, University of Bristol Press, 1984

Elizabeth Casson, Dorset House School of Occupational Therapy, 1930-1986

Frances Power Cobbe, *Life of Frances Cobbe as told by herself*, Swann Sonnenschein & Co., 1909

Jeremy & Margaret Collingwood, *Hannah More*, Lion Publishing Plc. 1990

Ed's. Madge Dresser & Philip Ollerenshaw, *The Making of Modern Bristol*, Redcliffe Press, 1996

Marguerite Fedden, Bristol Vignettes, The Burleigh Press, Bristol T.U.C., *A History of the T.U.C.*, 1968

David Foot, *Famous Bristolians*, Redcliffe Press, 1979

Winifred Gérin, *Elizabeth Gaskell*, Oxford University Press, 1980

F.G. Gross, *A Panorama of the Bristol Medical School*, University of Bristol Press, 1993

Ed. LM Hellstedt, *Women Physicians of the World*, 1978

Patricia Hollis, *Jennie Lee - A Life*, Oxford University Press, 1997

Hazel Holt, *A Lot to Ask, A Life of Barabara Pym,* Mac,illan, 1990

S Hutton, *Bristol and its Famous Associations*, JW Arrowsmith, 1907

Jo Manton, *Mary Carpenter and the Children of the Streets,* Heinemann Ed. Books Ltd, 1976

HE Meller, *Leisure and the Changing City*, Routledge and Kegan Paul, 1976

Marian Pease, *Some Reminiscences of University College*, Bristol, 1942 (unpublished MS)

Marian F Pease, *Notes on the Fry Family of Sutton Benger and Bristol* (MS)

Helen Reid, *A Chronicle of Clifton and Hotwells*, Redcliffe Press, 1992

Charles JG. Saunders, *The Bristol Royal Hospital for Sick Children*, Board of Governers of the United Bristol Hospital, 1960

Ed. Margaret J. Shoen, *Memorials of Two Sisters Susanna and Catherine Winkworth*, Longman, Green & Co., 1908

JB Thomas, *The Day Training College: a Victorian innovation in teacher training*, Bristol Journal of Teacher Education 4 (3), 1978. 249-61

F.M. Unwin, *Ada Vachell of Bristol*, J.W. Arrowsmith, 1928

Jean Vanes, *Apparelled in Red, The History of the Red Maids School*, The Red Maid's Scool, 1984

Mary Wright, *Elizabeth Blackwell of Bristol: The First Woman Doctor*, Bristol Branch of the Historical Association, 1995

Picture Credits

Index

Illustrations are denoted by page numbers in *italics*.